D1417690

DESERONTO PUBLIC LIBRARY

There was a time...

all the best

Roy Bonisteel

Other books

In Search of Man Alive
Man Alive: The Human Journey

DESERONTO PUBLIC LIBRARY

ROY BONISTEEL
There was a time...

Illustrations by Damian V. Glass

Doubleday Canada Limited

Copyright©1991 by Roy Bonisteel (text)
Copyright©1991 by Damian V. Glass (illustrations)

All rights reserved. No part of this publication may be repro-
duced, stored in a retrieval system, or transmitted, in any form
or by any means, electronic, mechanical, photocopying,
recording or otherwise, without the prior written permission of
Doubleday Canada Limited.

Canadian Cataloguing in Publication Data
  Bonisteel, Roy
    There was a time ...

ISBN 0-385-25298-6

1. Bonisteel, Roy. 2. Broadcasters - Canada - Biography. 3.
Religious broadcasting - Canada - Biography. I. Title.

PN4913.B6A3 1991   070.1'9'092   C90-095015-3

Typeset in Novarese Book on a Mac IIcx
Jacket design by Ross Mah Design Associates
Jacket photo by Johnnie Eisen

Printed on ∞ acid-free paper

Printed and bound in the USA

Published in Canada by Doubleday Canada Limited,
105 Bond Street, Toronto, Ontario, M5B 1Y3

To

Jessie, Siobhan, Emily, Drew,
Lauren, Kassia and Marley

For all time

Table of Contents

Preface

When my son Steven became an editor at the Kingston *Whig-Standard*, he asked me if I would consider writing a regular newspaper column. I said I didn't know what to write about.

"Just write about what it was like when you were a kid."

"Do you think anyone would find that interesting?"

"You must have thought I would," said Steve, "you told me about it often enough."

I guess I did. Hardly a day went by as Steve and his sisters Mandy and Lesley were growing up when I didn't refer to some time in my own childhood. To a young person I suppose it must have sounded like *Tales from the Stone Age*. To me it seemed just a short time ago. What helped to jog my memory and keep the nostalgic juices flowing was the fact that we often visited my parents in the farm area in which I was born. No matter what hill I climbed, what creek I crossed or what neighbour rode by on a hay wagon, the familiarity of the scene sparked a remembered tale.

My children were city kids, all born in St. Catharines, Ontario, in the late 1950s. For two years in the mid-sixties we lived in Vancouver, then four years in Toronto. At the dawning of the seventies I was becoming disillusioned with the educational programs being offered to my children in the big city. I couldn't see what all the regimentation, competition, tests, exams and homework had to do with developing interesting and caring human beings.

I've often said it was primarily this concern about my children's schooling that prompted our move to the farm. To be perfectly honest, it was much more than that. I was fed up with asphalt, freeway traffic and postage stamp lawns. I wanted to see the entire sky at night instead of a few patches peeking between high-rises and hydro towers. I wanted to taste fresh eggs and vegetables again, drink water from a spring or creek and hold once more a new-born foal or lamb in my arms. So, while I was reasonably sure a move to the country would be good for the kids, I knew it was essential for me.

It would cause few problems at work. It was 1971 and the television series "Man Alive," of which I was the host, was shot primarily on film. I only had to commute regularly once a week to package the program in the studio. Given that, it didn't really matter where I lived. I only needed to get to an airport and from there I could travel all over the world as the show demanded, just as I had been doing for four years.

No matter where the real estate signs led us we always seemed to end up in the Bay of Quinte area and so, when we heard the "Curtis place" was for sale, we didn't think twice. Actually a family named Harry lived there, but it had always been the Curtis place when I was a kid and so for me it remained so. Before my time it was known as the "Munn place." That's the way it is around here. It will be at least a century before people start calling it the "Bonisteel place."

As a boy I had lived only a mile down the road. I knew the school across the field, the church on the hill and of course the farm itself with its big double hip-roof house on the third concession of Sidney Township.

And I knew the people. Some of the farmers in the area had been old when I was a boy, and they were still there. Some had known my grandfather, all had known my mother and father and the ten Bonisteel kids including the youngest, Roy, who had grown up and become a newspaper reporter and then a broadcaster in radio and later on television.

For my children, Mandy, fourteen, Steven, twelve, and Lesley, eleven, it was the beginning of a new life riding horses, milking cows, ploughing fields, pitching hay and chopping wood. For me, forty-one, it was coming home.

Now, twenty years later, my son was suggesting I write about my early years and memories of this area.

"So, how often do I have to write these columns?" I asked.

"Once a week or once a month, whichever you like."

"I'm pretty busy with the show, maybe once a month makes more sense."

"OK. How about an almanac sort of approach? Think back and write about what it was like for you in January, or February or March. What did these months mean to you when you were growing up?"

Introduction

Introduction

When I look back at my boyhood years, I try not to gloss them over with a patina of rosy recollections. I don't want to evoke just the good memories. I try to distinguish between the smiles and the tears, the cheerful and the broken hearts.

My life as a boy was behind the times even as I lived it. In a world that was already motorized, electrified and vaccinated, our family was caught in a time warp of horse-and-buggy transportation, coal-oil-lamp illumination and home-brewed medicine. This has always made the distance between then and now seem even more remarkable to me. As the years roll by and my world changes, I often look back to ask myself what remains of that boy in overalls with manure on his boots. The answer comes readily enough in the old cliché that goes, "You can take the boy out of the country but you can't take the country out of the boy."

For me, circling the globe at amazing speed in search of a journalistic coup carries echoes of an exciting day-long trip across Lake Ontario. Interviewing the world's pre-eminent living theoretical physicist Stephen Hawking about black holes and quantum mechanics recalls lying on my back in a night-time pasture, wondering what kept the stars in place. Discussing theology with Mother Teresa or the Dalai Lama evokes the same unanswerable questions with which I pestered our simple rural pastor. Remembering the past is not just nostalgic. It's acknowledging where I've been so that I can see where I am.

When I moved back to the Bay of Quinte area in 1971 and settled my family on the old Curtis place, it didn't take long to pick up the vibrations of my earlier years. Some of my favourite country roads had been paved. Trenton and Belleville had gobbled up huge tracts of farm land. The air station had grown. But the people were as I remembered them.

The older farm families, contemporaries of my parents, simply treated me as the neighbour kid who had finally come to his senses and returned home. Their children, many of whom had taken over the running of the family farms, welcomed me as their close childhood friend who was once more back in their midst.

Visiting colleagues, who knew me only from Toronto or Vancouver, claimed I developed a split personality. They said I acted and talked differently when I trekked with them through the fields and woods of my farm than when I was in the city or on TV. According to them, I was quick to slip back in to the mannerisms and speech characteristics of my birthplace. Apparently the latter was especially noticeable when I was giving directions. "Back to Stirling," "across to Picton," "down to Napanee," "over to Consecon," "up to Brighton" and "out to the

Front," made absolute sense to me, but these expressions caused some very bemused reactions in my visitors. While expressions such as "somethin' else," "I'll d'ya," "Holy wah" and "wasn't that a hoot" may sound strange at Yonge and Bloor, they rolled off our tongues like "shit through a goose."

For some of my neighbours, it seemed time had stood still. One of our family's pleasures in the early years of my return was the keeping of a small apiary at the north end of the farm. Early one morning I spent some time at the hives before driving to Toronto to record some narration at the CBC. Since it's only an hour-and-a-half trip to the city, I was able to drive there and back, then return to the bees shortly after lunch. An old neighbour whom I had known all my life strolled over to where I was working and said, "I saw you back here early this morning, Roy."

"That's right," I answered. "I spent some time here before I went to Toronto."

"You went all the way up to Toronto today?" he asked with surprise. Without waiting for confirmation, he shook his head in wonder and reminisced, "I was up to Toronto once. Back in 1955. I went to that exhibition they have there." There was a long pause and then he added, "I never saw any reason to go back."

I liked the slower pace and the way at least part of my life was governed by the seasons once again. I liked the feeling of a close-knit community where doors were never locked, no one ever made appointments and you didn't need an excuse to drop in for a visit. I liked the way I could trade a few loads of hay for a side of beef or a neighbour would set a bucket of peas, fresh from the vine, on the front porch knowing I'd be dropping off a pail of honey later on in the year.

Today's family, whether urban or rural, bears little resemblance to the one in which I was raised. Yet, there are basic tenets and values that I think are worth recapturing and preserving.

My own childhood was spent in what I call loving neglect. No special attention was paid to me. With so many others in the family, I was rarely ever noticed, let alone doted on. We worked together, ate and slept together, played and laughed together. We were a large, noisy, healthy family of individuals, unfettered by much parental attention, mounting our own particular hobby-horses and riding madly off in all directions.

Only a generation ago, this was quite normal. Parents could not afford to invest too much emotional energy in any one infant; too many children died at birth or in the first four years of life. Today, in Canada, far more pregnancies are successful and nearly all children live. As parents have fewer children, they are more attached to each. Their hopes have narrower channels. We expect each child to be a precious, unique person. Our expectations are higher and, consequently, we are more disappointed when they miss the mark. As a young person starting out in life, it would have been very difficult for me to miss my parents' mark, because there wasn't one. Their expectations of me had nothing to do with occupation, achievement, position or honours. Their expectations of my brothers sisters and me had to do with more homely qualities – honesty, manners, civility, respect for others, compassion, fidelity and generosity.

Sociologists confirm that we are living in selfish times. They say we are shut up in our own inner space. It's an era dedicated to the cultivation of self and this great turning inward has become our new morality. As evidence they point to the bookstores where the get-ahead-by-intimidating-your-neighbour self-help books are such big sellers. These books promise power and guarantee success if one looks out for number one. It's all right according to these authors to be selfish, scheming or dishonest as long as you don't get caught at it. It's the fight of the solitary ego against other solitary egos.

Our consumer society reflects this catering to "me." We are being told on all sides to buy now, at any expense, whatever we want to fulfill our desires.

This pressure to indulge was not a factor in my growing-up years. If we wanted something, we either saved for it or did without. MasterCard, Visa and American Express were not around to grant instant gratification.

I believe this attitude of pampering and satisfying ourselves has many far-reaching effects. An example is our natural resources, which are being depleted at an alarming rate because we basically just care about ourselves – here and now – not tomorrow or the next generation, not even about others who are sharing this planet with us. Not caring about others seems to be the hallmark of today's society.

This has not always been so. In my boyhood

world you could not be selfish and survive. We depended on each other. I don't ever recall my parents or siblings telling me they loved me. They didn't have to. I knew I was loved because I was treated as an integral part of the family. I had responsibilities that had to be carried out on a daily basis. If not, other people would be adversely affected. Of course my family cared for me, because I was depended upon. I was important. In our modern labour-saving, electronically equipped, push-button households there's not much need for hard-working children, so we have to keep saying how much we love them or they'll never know.

I feel sorry for our youth of today. Many of them are underprivileged because they are over-privileged. With the best of intentions, parents strive to make it easy for their children. They are determined to give their offspring every advantage that they themselves did not have. The consequences are reported daily in the press and covered on the evening newscasts. In a country that takes pride in its great economic wealth, its advanced child-care system and its devotion to better quality life-styles, suicide is the second most common cause of death among teenagers.

I occasionally do guest broadcasts for CBC radio. These take the form of two- or three-minute pieces that are carried on several of the network's stations across Canada. Last year, after spending a few days in some high schools where I had been asked to speak, I returned home and thought about some of the kids I had met. I thought about the advantages they had compared to when I was their age.

I wrote and later broadcast the following comments:

I've been visiting high schools lately as part of a course on mass media and have met some fine young people. Kids you'd be proud to have in your home or for a son or daughter. I've met some other teenagers whom I find a great disappointment. A humourless lot who are fed up with life today and, when prodded a bit, will eventually tell you why.

They are bored, they say. Nothing interests them. They are angry with parents who don't understand them, hate school because "it's a waste of time" and couldn't care less about teachers who are "stupid."

"Come on," I say, "Things can't be that bad."

"Oh, yeah. What have we got to look forward to? The world is a sea of garbage. Our parents are only interested in making a buck. Our heroes turn out to be on steroids. Our politicians are all crooked, and don't talk to me about mass media — TV is just a crock of propaganda."

To those young people I met who are doing their best in school, enjoying each other and looking forward to the future, thanks for some interesting times. To the rest of you, let me say this: OK, so the world's not perfect, but you come across as a selfish, pampered lot. You are bored because you can't see beyond your own hang-ups. Take a look around you ... yes, at the garbage, at the loneliness, the suffering, the pain, then tell me there's nothing to do. You have no heroes or role models? Stop blaming Ben Johnson for *your* apathy. What he did was wrong, but at least he was in the race. You want heroes? Let me tell you about a girl named Callwood who despite personal tragedy, loss and harassment, spends every waking moment of her life ministering to the homeless, the destitute and the dying. Let me tell you about a Japanese boy named Suzuki whose earliest memories are of being behind barbed wire in a Canadian internment camp, who didn't stay bitter but became a leading scientist and is devoting his talents to saving not only our country, but our planet. Let me tell you about a young Ukrainian kid named Hnatyshyn who made up his mind to serve his country and the political system with distinction and who is now our twenty-fourth governor-general. Let me tell you about a one-legged guy named Fox who attempted to jog across the entire country and made it into our hearts to give us all a new meaning for the word courage.

Or even better, look around your community for role models. Our country is full of people who get up and go to work every day, even when they don't feel like it, so that kids like you can get an education, be healthy and enjoy the freedoms you take for granted.

You don't like TV? So, shut it off. Read a book or do something around your home to help out. And, remember this, the world does not owe you a living. You owe the world something. You owe it your time, your talent, your energy and your imagination so that no one need be hungry or afraid or lonely or sick. Get a sense of humour. Laugh at yourself, that's always a good place to start. Don't push people away. There are a lot of us who are cheering for you. There are a lot of us who love you ... and considering the fact that you're our future, there are a lot of us who are counting on you.

Do us all a favour ... and get yourself a life!

Following the broadcast, CBC radio received one of its highest number of requests ever for copies of a transcript. From Vancouver to Halifax, parents, teachers and the young people themselves wanted a permanent record of what I had said. In Edmonton alone, over a thousand listeners wrote for a copy, prompting the station to organize a public meeting between me and a hall full of local teenagers to discuss what had become known as "Bonisteel's Get a Life Editorial." The meeting was taped and broadcast on both TV and radio throughout Alberta. It was not the confrontation the organizers expected. The fact was, most of the teenagers there agreed with me. While some felt I should have been more critical of the parents, many admitted to a feeling of apathy caused by a lack of challenge. Television came in for a great deal of blame and rightfully so.

When I was the age of these Edmonton teen-agers, my community was bordered by a one-room school house, a rural country church and a co-op cheese factory. These formed a centre for our lives. In the television age the community is not just our neighbourhood; it's also "Mr. Rogers' Neighbour-hood" with a "Sesame Street" and a "Degrassi Street." It has "Twin Peaks" with a "Night Court" and a "Cheers" bar. Those closest to us are not the next-door neighbours or even members of our family but "Murphy Brown," "The Simpsons," "Rosanne" and the "Teenage Mutant Ninja Turtles." The make-believe, fantasy world of television commands nearly eight hours of the average young person's day. No wonder there's very little enthusiasm left for the trials and tribulations of the real world.

A number of years ago, I interviewed Elie Wiesel, poet, author, Nobel Peace Prize winner and survivor of both Buchenwald and Auschwitz. He talked about the need for silence in a world of constant noise. "In many ways," he said, "we are the most talkative generation in the world. We are obsessed with communication. So many newspapers, radios, televisions, that talk, talk, talk and say nothing. Very often it is what cannot be said that is important." He went on to explain that, although silence was to be cherished, there was indeed a time to break silence, a time to speak out and "be a witness."

"I see myself," he said, "as a witness to the past through tales and story-telling. I try to reach out, especially to the young, and say, 'Look what happened.' To live today is to remember. So, listen to my tales and spread them."

It seems to me the telling of tales is essential if we want to make this a better world for future generations.

In a society obsessed with self-indulgence and waste I like to recall a time when thrift and hard work were their own rewards. As our cities become choked with garbage and our air thick with smog, it's important to remember a time of sparkling streams and healthy forests. In an age when we assign our elderly to institutions or to "granny flats" in the back-yard next to the dog house, I think of old aunts who shared their wisdom and love in the family home. In a country where the GNP is our symbol for success, the BMW our sign of social status and where banks have replaced cathedrals as our tallest buildings, I like to tell stories of people of humble means who were rich in spirit.

When I first read Dickens, I used to wonder what he meant when he wrote, "It was the best of times, it was the worst of times. It was the age of wisdom, it was the age of foolishness." Now that I'm older I understand, because the lines fit every age. Yet, I can't help but feel there is a special challenge for all of us today, especially our youth. We have the opportunity, the knowledge and the resources to make things better and to create the kind of society that Dickens or my parents or myself as a young farm boy could only imagine. We lack for nothing ... except the will.

January

January

I guess everyone thinks there was more snow and ice and the wind was colder in days gone by. If they had lived here in the Quinte area, they would have been correct. And, you don't have to take my word for it or that of any of my neighbours I can show you photographic proof of snow-drifts that touched the telephone wires, hundreds of acres of buried fences and houses with snow piled to the second storey.

The Bay of Quinte is about three miles wide where it separates Bayside from the north shore of Prince Edward County. In January it accommodates ice fishermen and their huts along its edge. But when I was young, the entire bay was frozen solid from shore to shore.

Wrapped in buffalo robes and sheepskins, we would crowd into a cutter or bob-sled while our team of Percherons drew us rapidly across the bay.

You could skate for miles without any fear of thin ice or open water. Five or six of us would attach a large sheet of canvas to a couple of cedar poles and, by tightly gripping these home-made masts while holding our feet together, we would be swept at incredible speeds over the ice.

January days on my parents' farm were centred around the chores. It took most of the morning to milk the cows, feed and water all the livestock and clean out the stables. In a few short hours it would be time to do it all over again.

It seemed hard, unrelenting drudgery, and I guess it was. My older brothers and sisters had it harder than I did simply because as the youngest less was expected of me. But everyone had their responsibilities, including me.

My very earliest memory is of winter. I'm not sure how old I was, perhaps two or three. I still needed help with my buttons. I recall jumping out of bed and running as fast as my legs would carry me through the frigid rooms and stairways to the blessed warmth of the kitchen cookstove where my sisters or mother would help me get dressed. I remember a cotton waistband with dangling garters that fastened onto long brown stockings which required older fingers than mine to manoeuvre.

Today, in the dining room of my own farm, the old family cook-stove has a place of honour. I still load it up on particularly cold days and it never disappoints me. But it was used for much more than heat in those days. It was the main survival unit for the whole family.

It cooked all the food for a family of twelve. This could be accomplished because, thankfully, we were all seldom home at the same time. Nonetheless, the table always seemed crowded.

I never tasted store-bought bread, cakes or pies as long as I lived at home. My mother was not what you would call an exciting cook. I don't suppose she had time to do any more than the basics. Most everything was boiled or fried. Meat depended on whatever had been slaughtered lately and potatoes and bread came with every meal.

There were always two pots on the stove. One was filled with water that simmered gently throughout the day, always at the ready. The other was a large enamel teapot that never seemed to run dry, but could be pushed to the front of the stove for instant boiling whenever someone was brave enough to indulge. A reservoir at the end of the stove held about three gallons of water and was warm enough for washing hands, faces and dirty dishes. The "warming closet" across the top held food for late arrivals and for drying wet mittens, socks and scarves. Behind the stove was piled the split wood. A cold January night would see a six-foot pile disappear. After supper, cedar kindling would be arranged on the open oven door to dry in preparation for the morning fire-starting.

The stove-pipes made their way into almost every room of the house, bringing a modicum of heat during the night, but never enough. Since there was no plumbing in the house, freezing was never a big problem. Many a winter morning the chamber-pot under the bed had a solid lid of ice. Creating holes in the ice was one of my favourite childhood diversions.

The stove brought the family together. The sheer need to keep warm kept us within its circle of heat. Hardly a winter evening passed when we weren't busy stoking up the fire for popcorn, fudge, taffy or hot cider. Many an orphan lamb, calf or piglet clung to life while snug beside it. Many a home-made poultice for human or animal was brewed on its top.

As I look at it now in my dining room, I realize it must be close to a hundred years old. It looks as good as ever. It has outlived my parents and five of my brothers and sisters. There's no doubt it will also survive me.

The stove is not the only survivor that furnishes my home. There is hardly a room in my farm house that doesn't contain some silent reminder of the past – a rocking chair, a table, a cupboard, my parents' double bed and even the quilt on the bed. These are all links to an earlier time and a testimony to endurance.

Even though they clash with more modern furnishings and present a decor that would drive an interior decorator crazy, they will never be thrown out. Hopefully, my children and grandchildren will find corners in their homes for them in years to come and the memories will continue.

Often, at the end of a year or the beginning of a new one, I like to reminisce. Sitting in Aunt Et's pine rocker in front of the old wood stove, with its fire-box turning a cosy red, helps me keep my life in perspective. No matter what successes or failures the past year has brought, they are of little significance in the long haul of history.

It's like sitting with old friends who "knew you when ...," have seen it all and will still be there for you when next New Year's rolls around.

OUT OF WORK

Comedian Jack Benny used to say that his idea of the perfect New Year's Eve celebration was to set his alarm clock for midnight, then when it rang, stick his head out of the window, shout "Happy New Year" to the world and go back to bed.

He likely said that to add to his parsimonious reputation, but I've always thought it was a sensible way to welcome the New Year. Blowing horns, throwing streamers and dancing till dawn at some over-priced fête can leave you in poor condition to ponder the past or plan for the future.

I like to spend the time looking back over the years counting what blessings have come my way. Then I picture the days ahead as an expanse of new-fallen snow where you can make your own fresh tracks. Granted, the conditions under which we live and the obligations we bear will dictate where some of those tracks lead, but there is always room to make our own individual impressions in that virgin territory.

I remember when the year 1950 was in its final days. I was quite a depressed twenty-year-old. I had been laid off from a job in a lumber yard that Christmas and faced the new year with no prospects except doing chores for room and board on the family farm. I was eligible for unemployment insurance benefits, but my father had a thing about "taking handouts from the government." He ranted and raved so much about baby bonuses, welfare cheques and pension schemes that none of us dared apply. Since his attitude softened later when he became eligible for senior citizens' benefits, I surmise he was just upset by the Liberal St. Laurent government of the day.

On the 30th of December I went to Trenton and made the rounds of businesses where I might possibly find employment. At the stores I heard that January was dead as far as sales were concerned. At the hotels I was told I had to be twenty-one to sling beer, although they'd be happy to sell me a draught in the spirit of the season. Finally I found a taxi company in need of extra drivers for New Year's Eve and since I already had my chauffeur's licence (which most farm boys had in those days) I could start driving on the 6:00 p.m. to 8:00 a.m. shift the next night. I found out later one had to be twenty-one to get a cab driver's licence, too, but the matter never came up.

At noon on the 31st a sleet storm began. When I reported for work that evening, Trenton and environs were forming a slushy, slippery skating rink and it was getting worse as the temperature dropped. Two cars of the eight-vehicle fleet were already out of commission through collisions and frozen gas lines. All available tire chains were in use and the only car left for me was a brand new 1951 Oldsmobile that the company owner had bought for himself.

I considered myself a fairly good driver behind the wheel of my Dad's ancient Nash or the Fargo farm truck, but I gave a nervous shiver when the dispatcher handed me the keys and said, "It's the boss's pride and joy and he hasn't had a chance to enjoy it yet. Be careful out there."

The fares were easy to memorize. There was a set rate for all trips. In-town trips and ones to the air base were one dollar. Belleville was set at two-fifty, Picton at four dollars and Kingston at eight dollars. The price

DESERONTO PUBLIC LIBRARY

was the same no matter how many squeezed in. As the night wore on and the icy streets became covered with a treacherous dusting of snow, I had the feeling everyone in the world was taking a cab and most of them seemed to be in mine.

The first half of my shift was an ordeal of spinning wheels, scraping the windshield, finding street addresses and making change. After midnight, not only was my cab loaded, but so were my passengers. Now I was lifting people in and out, fighting off cups of good cheer and expected to join in the hundredth singing of "Auld Lang Syne." Thankfully, the car's swerving and skidding seemed to increase their merriment. After the car hit an icy patch on Mountainview Hill and slid all the way to the bottom sideways, five whooping and cheering airmen insisted I should take up flying.

Somehow I got through the night. At eight in the morning of New Year's Day, I dumped my receipts and the car keys on the dispatcher's desk. He went outside the office and looked at the Oldsmobile. It was spattered with ice, muddy snow and what looked like vestiges of pink champagne, but miraculously had no dents or scratches. "You can start full-time if you want," he said. I really wasn't sure, but I thankfully accepted.

Looking back I guess it wasn't such a bad New Year's after all. I had a job and in the months ahead was able to make some tracks of my own with new experiences and interesting people. That's a good wish to extend to everyone at the beginning of any year.

I remember a phrase that used to describe a person travelling fast, either on horseback or in a vehicle, which claimed, "He was coming down the road like sixty." This meant the person seemed to be going at sixty miles per hour and the statement was understood to be an obvious exaggeration. Anyone going that slowly now can expect to be hooted off the road.

When I was a boy, I lived next to the Trenton Air Base and used to watch the Harvards and Cessnas swoop through the sky at what I thought was incredible speed. I never guessed that in my lifetime a giant aircraft called the Concorde would one day land there after crossing the Atlantic in only three and a half hours.

As I sit in the corner of my home, surrounded by a word processor, printer, fax machine, photo-copier, and portable push-button telephone, I am in awe. I certainly would not have dreamt that any of these would come to pass.

When I review the predictions that I do remember over the years, I'm just as happy I was never tempted to make any.

PREDICTIONS

We have all had a few days now to digest the many expert predictions that are made at this time of year, designed to chart our course for the next year, the next decade and beyond. Some are exciting and challenging; others are scary and apocalyptic. All should be taken with a few grains of the proverbial salt.

Predictions as to what lies ahead are a New Year's tradition. Long ago I gave up on them ever coming true.

"Nuclear-powered vacuum cleaners will be a reality within ten years." (Alex Lewyt, manufacturer, 1955.)

Why intelligent people in business, medicine, sports or science make definite statements about the future, I'll never figure out. How must they feel when their prognostications are proven wrong? Of course some don't stay around to find out.

"My figures coincide in fixing 1950 as the year the world must go smash." (Henry Adams, U.S. historian, 1836-1918.)

At the beginning of every year, the media give space and time to astrologers telling us where we and our planet are headed. They use the scatter-gun approach, making hundreds of predictions in the belief that some will be right. Nostradamus, the daddy of pop astrology, did the same thing back in the 1500s and spawned the Jeanne Dixons of today. It's harmless as long as we don't live our lives according to the position of Pluto.

"Airplanes will never carry more than five to seven passengers." (Waldeman Kaemfort, editor, *Science America Magazine*, 1913.)

When I was a boy *Flash Gordon* was a popular comic strip. Each week I followed the adventures of Flash, his girlfriend Dale and Dr. Zarchov as they travelled through the future fighting off the enemies of civilization. I thought how wonderful it would be to visit some planet and be home for supper or zoom off to school with a battery-powered backpack that lifted you over the barns and trees. Maybe someday we will, but I'm glad I didn't waste my time waiting for it.

"Television won't be able to hold onto any market it captures after the first six months. People will soon get tired of staring at a plywood box every night." (Daryl F. Zanuck, film producer, 1946.)

It's normal to wonder about the future and even speculate what 1991 holds for us. Will the economy improve? Will the free trade deal work? Will *glasnost* continue? Will I get a raise and be able to afford a new car? Some answers will come from our own individual efforts and some are out of our control, but all will be the result of a day-by-day pilgrimage into the future. None will be decided by any one expert.

"I *think there is a world market for about five computers.*" (Thomas J. Watson, chairman of IBM, 1943.)

Eight years ago our family bought a VCR machine when the price was three times what it is today. We were warned that with increased production, more competition and greater availability of home videos the price would drop drastically. But compare the hours of pleasure we've had over the years to the timidity of those who are convinced that price will go even lower.

A neighbour I know sold his farm at a cut-rate price because his religious leader prophesied the world would end in 1975. The date has now been moved up and he sits waiting in his rented apartment. A young couple told me recently they had no intention of having children because the future of our ecosystem was so bleak.

The sad part about believing in forecasters and speculators is the time we lose savouring today. This hour of our lives is the most valuable, and one of the great joys of living each day at a time is the sweet mystery of the future.

"Yesterday is a cancelled cheque; tomorrow is a promissory note; today is the only cash you have — so spend it wisely." (Florence Bonisteel, my mother.)

February

February

Along with the daily chores, winter days also meant felling trees in the woods and sawing them into cordwood lengths for stacking and seasoning. It was also a time to haul the manure from the piles near the barn for spreading on the fields. Both of these important farm jobs had to be accomplished before the snow became too deep for the horses and sleigh to negotiate. This happened regularly every winter. It simply meant we were "snowed in."

Nowadays being snowed in means that perhaps for one day during the winter the school bus doesn't run or a sidestreet is closed for snow removal. When it happened on the farm in the thirties and forties, it meant being completely marooned for several weeks. No phone, no mail, no snow-plough.

For me it meant no school. There was no way I could walk three miles through snow that was well over my head. It also meant helping to dig a way out to the barn to feed the animals, clearing snow off the creek and chopping watering holes. I spent the rest of the time in the house, snug by the stove, reading everything I could get my hands on.

I don't remember when I learned how to read, but it must have been before I started school since I recall how bored I was with *Mary, John and Peter*. That was the name of our grade one primer. Mary, John and Peter were siblings who kept running up to their dog and saying, "Hurry, hurry, come and see the big green apple on my tree." I was constantly getting into trouble for skipping to the back of the book where at least the stories had a plot. I also liked the poetry at the back of the book. One simple little verse went:

> An icicle hung on a red brick wall,
> And it said to the sun,
> I don't like you at all,
> Drip, drip, drip.

We did not have a school library, only the prescribed books for each grade. Sometimes I would smuggle home books from the older kids. This was easy to accomplish since all eight grades were in the same room. I would discover words I had never heard or seen before and explore worlds I longed to see. These books were special treasures because we had a limited number of books at home and were without the resources to buy new ones. Consequently, once I learned how to read well, it didn't take many "snowed in" winters to go through our supply.

One year we couldn't leave the farm for nearly a month. The old horse-drawn wooden snow-plough made several attempts to get down our road without success. Food was not a problem since we had our own canned goods and staples. The flour and sugar were always purchased in hundred-pound bags well before winter. Water, however, was in short supply.

The creek had frozen completely and what water we could coax from the well was needed for the live-stock. It was a winter I remember well since during that month we had to thaw tubs of snow and ice to wash clothes and take baths. My brother carved a huge propeller out of a cedar rail to make a wind-charger so we could recharge the wet-cell battery that ran our radio, and I, starved for anything on a printed page, read the Holy Bible from cover to cover.

THE DARK ROOM

We had a "dark room" in our old family farmhouse and it had nothing to do with photography. I remember it as a sanctuary from the frustrations of February.

The only good thing about February is its length. The festive season is long past, the pristine beauty of snow and ice grows tiresome. With every croupy breath we ache for spring. The dark room, or equivalent, is a child's only escape.

The house had no attic. All the bed-rooms had sloping ceilings and were situated either over the kitchen or the parlour to take advantage of the stove-pipes that provided what little nocturnal warmth there was. In the centre of the upstairs, sealed off to prevent drafts, was a wide, window-less room separating the girls' side from the boys' side. It was called the dark room and was used for storage. Old bedsteads, broken rockers, used mattresses, pieces of harness, clothes, boxes, trunks and chests made a jungle of possibilities for exploration and discovery.

Many a boring February day found me with flashlight or lantern sorting many years of accumulated family jetsam. Most of the stuff came from departed relatives. When some great aunt or second cousin "slipped these mortal coils," their worldly goods were divided among the grieving survivors and usually a crate or two ended up in our dark room.

By the time I reached the age of curiosity and cunning, the room contained wall-to-wall relics and I was able to escape winter chores by the hour without rummaging through the same trove twice. The rest of the family just assumed I was outside playing somewhere. After all, who in their right mind would want to spend time in a cold, musty, unlit garret?

One day I was poking around in a corner of the room under the eaves when I came across a cardboard box bound with twine. Crayonned on its side was, "Uncle Henry's Things."

This was rather surprising because great Uncle Henry had died before I was born and I knew that his things were already scattered throughout the house. One of our beds had been his. The amazing Edison gramophone, several rockers and a washbowl set had all come our way after the funeral. But, for me, the most important inheritance had been several dozen books, which by this time I had read and reread. Rudyard Kipling, Bret Harte, James Fenimore Cooper and T. E. Lawrence had all been favourites of Uncle Henry and were my introduction into new and wonderful worlds.

Although I had never met the man, I knew what he looked like. Relatives as generous as he got their pictures hung on the parlour wall. Plump face, pince-nez glasses with a black ribbon attached, a large walrus moustache that drooped to touch a high celluloid collar gave him a remarkable resemblance to Teddy Roosevelt.

I pried the binding off the corners of the box and opened it up. Wonder of wonders, more books, and what exciting titles: *Tales of the Decameron*, the *Kama Sutra*, *The Perfumed Garden* and several books by another

Lawrence. This one's initials were D.H.

I propped the flashlight up on a pile of blankets and began to read. After a few pages I understood why my parents, unable to destroy or throw away books of any kind, had simply decided to segregate them from our communal reading material. It never occurred to them that the books would be discovered in their dark-room hiding place by a young lad bored with February.

Hours later I heard someone calling me for supper and I made my way out of the dark room with a head full of images and the knowledge that I would spend many more afternoons in that cramped corner with my hidden cache. There was no reason to tell anyone. It would just be my secret. But when I walked past Uncle Henry's picture in the parlour, I could have sworn behind the moustache and glasses I glimpsed a smile and a wink.

With the exception of the kitchen, every room in the old farmhouse was decorated with pictures of long-deceased relatives. These sombre men and women, caught stiffly in time by a flash of light that would preserve their image forever, stared down at me as though waiting to be released from their pose.

Captured in huge gilt frames that hung by long copper wires from the ceiling mouldings, they were a source of much youthful curiosity.

"Tell me again who that is," I would urge my mother.

"That's your great-grandmother Eliza Finkle on your father's side."

"What's that on her head?"

"It's a lace cap trimmed with taffeta. A lot of women wore them when they got older because their hair had started to thin. It kept their heads warm."

"What's she holding?"

"It's just a piece of cardboard. When photographers took your picture in those days, they insisted you hold something. No one knew what to do with their hands, so you were given a piece of paper, a book or even a glove to hold."

The portraits of married couples always had the husband sitting, legs crossed, grasping the arms of a high-backed chair. The wife stood tall and proud off to one side with her hand on his shoulder. If children were present, they sat in starched crinolines or sailor suits at father's feet.

My mother managed to reserve a corner of the parlour, away from our ancestors, to hang a remarkable four-by-five-foot print of Rosa Bonheur's *The Horse Fair*. This masterpiece of rearing wild-eyed steeds against a background of sky and trees, was so life-like and powerful that I used to sit and study it for hours. Many years later I was thrilled to see the original in the Metropolitan Museum of Art in New York, where it had been donated by Cornelius Vanderbilt.

In a secluded hallway nook hung a delicate watercolour on enamel, which had a fascinating story. I would beg for its telling again and again. It too came from Uncle Henry's "things" and was supposedly painted by his son Blake Hunt, after his premature death. Blake Hunt had been an amateur artist with a penchant for water scenes bordered by leafy trees, misty mountains and a few V-shaped flocks of birds on the wing. A victim of the influenza epidemic following the First World War, he died in his late twenties and his mother, devastated by sorrow, sought solace in spiritualism. After several visits to a well-known Toronto medium, she finally made contact with "the other side" and Blake responded through table rapping, suspended trumpets, mechanical writing and pencil drawings on slate. One glorious day, the desperate mother was presented with complete proof of her son's continued existence in the form of a beautiful scene in lush watercolour on enamel that captured every nuance of Blake's former work.

"Do you believe this could actually happen?" I would ask my mother.

"It doesn't really matter whether we believe it or not," she would answer for the hundredth time. "Your Aunt Sophronia believed it and this brought her a great deal of comfort."

"But how could a painting be sent back from the dead?"

"It's not up to us to question the faith of others. Some people walk by faith, not sight, and see life and death as an unexplained mystery. Wherever the picture came from, I find it quite lovely."

The painting, still in its original gold frame, now hangs in my house over a small tintype of Blake taken shortly before his death.

Pictures of the immediate family never hung on the walls in the old farmhouse. The collection consisted of snapshots, kept in photo albums and held in place by little sticky paper corners. There are baby pictures of my seven older brothers and sisters, but none of the three youngest – Bert, Flossie or me.

Today, when a magazine writer asks for early boyhood poses to illustrate an article, I'm forced to admit, "I'm sorry I don't have any. You see, that was around the time Dad went into purebred Holsteins."

In the thirties, the Holstein-Friesian Association required two side-view pictures of a new-born calf before registering the animal. This would prove that there was an equal proportion of white to black, no black below the knees and no black on the switch part of the tail – all strict requirements for purebred status. As our herd grew in number, our Brownie box-camera was much in demand and the cost of film and processing precluded its use for anything as frivolous as taking pictures of children. Consequently, our photo albums from that period have plenty of pictures of calves, a few prize-winning bulls and some farm machinery but seldom any evidence of human life. Now and again, in the background, peeking around the corner of the barn, you can see a child straining desperately to get into the shot but they are so far in the distance, identification is impossible.

I discovered one early picture of me, obviously taken at a family reunion, among discarded out-of-focus and head-cropped prints in an old shoe box. There, in the front row, surrounded by brothers, sisters and assorted cousins, is a curly-haired two-year-old, either so bored by the proceedings or so unused to having his picture taken that he has his hand down the front of his pants. The picture never made it into any album.

Scrapbooks were very popular and almost every family member kept one. I still have one I assembled in 1939 of the king and queen's visit to Canada. Another one contains my collection of movie stars, with several pages devoted to Shirley Temple, who was the same age as me. Another is full of favourite poems, letters from pen-pals and dozens of cherished valentines.

VALENTINES

This is the month when the windows of our elementary schools blossom with hearts, cupids and bits of paper lace. The February ritual of folding, cutting and pasting red and white poster paper has been around a long time.

At old School Section Number Four we used to look forward to St. Valentine's day with excitement. It gave us the opportunity to find out who liked whom the most. It wasn't the number of cards that counted, since the "great exchange" meant that everyone gave to everyone else. It was the wording on the messages that told the tale.

"Agnes likes me more because she says her heart beats only for me. On yours it just says, 'Be my valentine.'"

The teacher's card was always an important one. It was usually store-bought and had a little bend-out foot at the back that allowed it to stand up by itself. If her message said something like, "You are special to me, valentine," you thought you had it made.

The observance of St. Valentine's day faded rather rapidly after about grade three, except perhaps a card for mother, grandmother or the neighbour with the cookies. The day didn't become important again until around the first year of high school when you met THE ONE. I don't just mean the cute kid in the third row in chemistry or the one that let you copy her Latin homework. I mean the dry throat, rubber knees ONE.

For her you spent hours dreamily searching for that perfect card even if it cost a dollar. No childish little cardboard cut-out was good enough. We wanted those lacy ones with fat lavender hearts that stuck out from the card like satin pillows. No more of that "My heart beats 4 U" stuff. We had to have messages that used words like "forever," "eternity" or phrases like "till the oceans run dry." We might even write our own valentine poem borrowing heavily from Browning, Shelley or "The Rubaiyat of Omar Khayyam."

As we grew older and realized that the love affair of all time happened every few months, St. Valentine's day again lost a lot of impact.

Its charm was recaptured only when our children started bringing home their February projects to decorate the refrigerator door.

Back before Hallmark cornered the market, valentines commonly were penny postcards mailed to friends and relatives in great number. I found some in a collection of old cards in a family album. They were used for more than just professing love. They were apparently social commentaries. One I have, dated 1909, shows a dejected cupid in front of a bank and the message:

> The rose is red —
> the violet's blue,
> but these I do not send to you.
> Because just now
> the times are hard,
> so I will send this postal card.

I have the impression that St. Valentine's day is not the big deal it once was. With postage stamps costing forty cents and boxes of chocolates not the most popular gifts for weight-conscious lovers, the day tends to slip by unnoticed. I'm pleased to see that it is still kept alive by the younger school children. I think it's nice to have a time in the calendar dedicated to love. And what better month than February, a desolate month that celebrates nothing else of significance except a day for groundhogs?

March

March

I should try to give you a picture of the farm where I grew up. It was one hundred acres between the first and second concessions of Sidney Township on what was called "the Blind Second." This was a dead-end road that actually came to a halt in our driveway. We couldn't see neighbours on either side although their farms abutted ours. Two railway tracks, the CPR and the CNR (formerly the Grand Trunk) ran east and west across our fields.

The phrase "mixed farming" has come to mean an operation where several agricultural enterprises are carried on at the same time and a little money is made from each. In our case we tried every farming operation ever designed, with no real profit from anything.

First was the dairy herd. These were the days before milk contracts, electric milkers, refrigerated milk parlours or tank-truck pick-up. We milked twenty to thirty cows by hand morning and night. Spring, summer and fall the milk was taken every day by horse and wagon, later by truck, to the local cheese factory about four or five miles away. In the winter, since the milk supply was less plentiful, it was brought into the house and put through the cream separator. The skimmed milk was fed to the pigs and the cream churned for our butter and buttermilk.

Side by side with the cows were the horses. We always had more horses than we really needed to work the farm since my father had a fondness for them. He had quite a reputation in the area as a horse breeder and trainer and often showed the animals at Ontario fairs and exhibitions.

Along with the inevitable array of calves, foals and lambs we had pigs, sheep, chickens, geese, turkeys, ducks and their offspring. In order to feed all this livestock, most of the fields, made rich from the animal manure, would be planted with hay, wheat, corn, oats and barley, which of course had to be harvested, threshed, stored or ground before it could be consumed. This set up an exhausting cycle of work that as far as the animals were concerned just produced food that went in one end and out the other.

Most successful farmers concentrate on one aspect of agriculture and devote all their efforts to its profitable management. This was not the Bonisteel way. We seemed to try everything, and all at the same time.

We had a good-sized orchard, but hardly two trees of the same variety. While the market was hot for McIntosh or Delicious apples, we were experimenting with strains called Wealthy, Wolf River, Transparent, Bottle Greening, Duchess and a hybrid with a banana flavour called Melba. We had a few trees each of Blue Damson plums, Montmorency cherries and Bartlett pears. Dad was the only farmer in the Quinte area ever to grow peaches and grapes successfully, since our frigid winters supposedly made the raising of tender fruit crops impossible. It wasn't that he planned on making any money from them. It's just that he wanted to prove it could be done.

For a couple of years we did turn a profit on raspberries. I remember every member of the family, plus a horde of local teenagers (who were paid five cents a quart) picking the delicious red Cuthberts and Lathams from morning till night. We would then load the boxes in tall wooden crates and drive them to the train station in Trenton for shipment to Montreal. I'm not sure why we didn't continue the raspberry business. Perhaps the market changed or, more likely, it was the year Dad decided his future was in pumpkins.

He kept bees for a while and we enjoyed giving away most of the honey. Then he turned to guinea-fowl, those strangely speckled scrawny-necked birds that sleep in trees and scream, "buckwheat ... buckwheat" when they're hungry. Sheep became a passion even though we never had proper fencing and they close-cropped most of the pasture away from the cows and horses. He couldn't decide between the handsome black-faced Shropshires or the homely Roman-nosed, shaggy-wool Leicesters, so he raised both. March was shearing month. At a young age I was taught where to press on sheeps' throats to render them immobile while my brothers turned the cranks that powered the shears my father guided over the trembling bodies to remove the winter's harvest of lanoline-soaked wool.

It was not a job I liked and it certainly was not nearly as much fun or as romantic as "boiling down."

MAPLE SYRUP

There is a teen-age quality about March — restless, rebellious, full of unpredictable urges. The time the sap begins to rise.

Warm days and cold nights have been the recipe for perfect sugar bush weather for ages. Forty gallons of sap for one gallon of syrup is the equation for the blissful sweet tooth.

I read once that the sugar or hard maple was the most important tree in North America. It makes some of the finest furniture, provides the best shade and is startlingly beautiful when decked in autumn's scarlet and yellow. But in March it does what no other tree can do — provide streams of clear, delicious nectar that when first evaporated must surely have seemed the fabled ambrosia of the gods.

My father's sugar bush was part of our forty-acre woods. It was a magical place for a young boy any time of year, but especially on the day we "tapped." The huge black iron kettle, which was used at other times of the year for scalding the bristles off slaughtered hogs, was loaded on the horse-drawn farm sleigh and taken to the open pit in a sheltered part of the bush. Next came the buckets and the spikes, tapered tubes of metal with a small hole at the narrow end and a hook under the lip end. Dad handled the brace and bit, boring a neat three-quarter-inch hole in the tree about four feet from the slushy ground. My brother would hammer in the spikes with a wooden mallet and I would hang the long slim buckets. Within seconds the dripping sap would drum a tattoo off the tin bottom. The other trees soon echoed the beat.

If the tree was over two feet thick, a bucket could be hung on both sides. One huge old giant on the edge of the creek proudly supported six buckets that overflowed twice a day. The sleigh was too big and cumbersome to manoeuvre between the trees, so one horse was hitched to a smaller "stone boat" that skidded through the snow, carrying the milk cans full of sap to the steaming kettle. Pine stumps made the hottest fuel and it was nearly a full-time job to feed the roaring fire.

The best part was at night. Boiling down was a twenty-four-hour job.

Once you started, there was no stopping until the liquid began to turn amber and thicken. All night long the sap was added, the fire stoked and the bubbling brew skimmed with a long-handled strainer to remove the bits of bark, leaves and suicidal bugs.

The sound of the woods at night is soft – a swish of wind high in the upper most branches, a gurgle from the stream a few hundred feet away, the sputter of fire when it hits a damp spot on a log. It's a delight for any boy to be allowed to stay up all night, but to spend those dark mysterious hours in the March woods by a boiling sap kettle is sheer joy.

When I was twelve we went modern, at least for those days. The black kettle was relegated permanently to the pigs and a shiny new sap pan, eight feet by four feet by eight inches deep, was taken into the bush for the first time. Now the sap collected in two weeks could be boiled down in one final night with the fire banked under the entire bottom of this huge pan. The "men" were no longer needed all night to cut the wood and carry the heavy cans of sap. All that was required was someone to skim the syrup, keep a watchful eye on it and douse the fire if the syrup became low enough in the pan to "catch." I did it perfectly for two glorious years, and then disaster struck.

I had built a makeshift lean-to of birch saplings and covered them with a worn canvas from the grain binder to keep out the odd night shower. Pine boughs and an old sheepskin made a comfortable floor to lie on and read by firelight from my cache of pulp westerns. I don't know if it was the sweet stillness of the spring night, the heavy burden of being fourteen or the simple frontier tales by Max Brand and Luke Shortt that put me to sleep. I only know that around 3:00 a.m. I awoke with a chill that had nothing to do with the weather. It was my nose that told me first. A small portion of the pan was showing through the dark liquid and that smell of scorching syrup has been with me ever since.

Fourteen days of hard work, two hundred gallons of sap had come to this ignoble end.

Oh, we salvaged most of it. My mother stored it in mason jars and lined them up on the cellar shelf as usual. But for the rest of the year, I could not escape the accusing glances from my family as they chewed their morning pancakes now flavoured with a new pungency.

The world may remember 1944 as the year of the European invasion, or the year that saw Bing Crosby and *Going My Way* win Academy Awards, but in the annals of Bonisteel family history, it was the year Roy scorched the maple syrup.

A trip to the sugar bush is a spring highlight for many school children today. They see miles of plastic tubing connecting the trees to large efficient evaporators simmering over a controlled heat source.

Neither sap nor syrup is exposed to bark nor bug. Pure maple syrup is still a delicious natural food, but sometimes I miss the dark, smoky tang that speaks of March nights in snowy woods, blazing pine stumps and teen-age folly.

Living off the land had many advantages when it came to meal planning, the main one being there was hardly ever a shortage of food. Hard work in the outdoors meant hearty appetites and our large family sat down to a bountiful repast three times a day.

Breakfast was usually oatmeal or cracked wheat porridge, using our own freshly milled grain, eggs and side pork with fried potatoes and home-made bread. I'm not sure what a modern dietician would think of this for the first meal of the day, but it should be borne in mind that we had already done two or three hours of work.

Dinner was at noon – potatoes again, usually boiled. The meal included meat and whether it was beef, pork or mutton depended on what had been recently slaughtered. Vegetables could be of any variety and there was always some kind of dessert. Apple sauce, maple syrup, bread pudding and fruit pies were popular, usually accompanied by wedges of cheese or thick fresh cream.

Supper was around five o'clock. It was largely made up of leftovers from dinner, typically because everyone in the family worked in the fields up until early evening. This time, the previously boiled potatoes were chopped up with onions, seasoning and chunks of bread. The result tasted something like the stove-top stuffing we see packaged in the stores today.

While there was always an abundance of food, it was prepared simply with no pretence to *haute cuisine*. The Sunday chicken, for example, was always boiled. It was always one of the old non-producers that had been culled from the flock and was certainly too tough for the roasting pan.

I have never been a finicky eater and I attribute this to my early mealtime experiences which were simply dedicated to filling my stomach. I was never forced to eat anything by parental command. I either ate the food that was on the table or went hungry. As a result, I developed a fondness for certain dishes that seem to repel young people today. Turnips, squash, liver, Brussels sprouts, tongue, boiled cabbage, head cheese and buttermilk are as welcome on my dining-room table today as they were on the farm kitchen table of my youth.

I'm pleased to notice, in recent years, a trend to recapture the delights of self-sufficiency in food. Garden plots are now springing up in city and suburban yards as people discover the superior taste of home-grown vegetables and the satisfaction of preserving and storing produce for out-of-season use. It is a practice I have always followed, no matter where I've lived, not only for the pleasure it provides but to enhance the sense of being part of the food chain that sustains and nourishes us all.

WHISTLING

My squash is starting to squish. It must be March.

Those of us who enjoy gardening and store some of our vegetables over the winter know that March is the month to cart the remains out to the compost heap.

Those golden turnips of last fall are turning slightly grey, the carrots are showing a tendency to bend and the potatoes are beginning to put forth little shoots from every eye. There may be a last-minute soup or ragout reprieve for some of them, but the warmer weather has taken its toll.

By means of an air pipe to the outside, a section of my basement known as the cold room maintains a fairly constant temperature of about fifty degrees. This not only keeps my root vegetables in delicious shape but also assures that my home-made wine is always ready for immediate quaffing. Alas, unlike wine, vegetables do not improve with age but are destined to become nutrients for next year's crops.

Compared to the old days, I actually store very little. A couple of crates of potatoes, a dozen or so squash and a garbage can full of carrots constitute my winter provender.

Some people call their cold rooms root cellars, but to me a cellar must have an earthen floor, not concrete, no heat source or cement block walls and should be damp and musty.

The cellar of my parents' old farmhouse was the full size of the building. The floor was smoothly packed clay and the walls were thick stone chinked with plaster and mud. At this time of year thawing ice and spring rain would trickle through the stones and flood the floor with three or four inches of dirty, cold water. Thick planks floated like rafts on the surface and became slippery paths when one tried to get to the produce. Since we had no refrigerator or

DESERONTO PUBLIC LIBRARY

freezer, the cellar was our only place to store food and, with a family of twelve, was a very important part of the house. It was our family's lifeline for a good half of the year.

Piles of turnips, beets, carrots and squash, in bins partially filled with earth, lined one side of the room. The other was taken up by one huge bin for potatoes. Mountains of Irish Cobblers, Kenebec and Sebago provided the main diet for a farm family that often saw potatoes on the menu for each of the three daily meals.

Hanging from wires stretched across the ceiling were cabbages with roots attached, kohlrabi, bags of onions and sheaves of dried mint and catnip for tea. In the middle of the cellar was a forty-gallon wooden barrel of apple cider, which worked away all winter long and by March had made its inevitable progress from a belly-warming snort to a fairly decent vinegar.

Shelves on two sides bent under the weight of hundreds of mason jars filled with preserved beans, corn, stewed tomatoes, relish, peaches, plums, pears, jams and several kinds of pickles. There were crocks of home-made butter and rendered lard and a couple of sixty-pound rounds of cheese, which aged and grew more interesting over the winter months.

It was a veritable supermarket of staple foods and delicacies just a few feet away from the kitchen.

My mother didn't like going into the cellar. It was dark, the floating planks were tricky to traverse and it was home for several mice that had come in from the cold and stayed for the banquet. We kids were the ones who were sent to "go fetch." That is why, at a very early age, we were all taught how to whistle.

The instructions were something like this: "I need a dish of butter, a jar of ginger tomatoes and a basket of potatoes, so pucker up!" Our parents knew that as long as they could hear us whistle we weren't sampling a syrupy jar of cling peaches, stealing a slab of cheese or, depending on our age, siphoning a fast sip from the cider barrel.

I'm sure the quality of the food from my freezer and refrigerator is much better now, and for the most part the hard labour of preserving and storing is in the past, but one thing remains. When I go down to my basement to clear out the remnants of my meagre crop, I'll likely be whistling. Old habits die hard.

Growing food, harvesting crops and storing the produce comes naturally to me. The Bonisteels have always been farmers.

Originally they farmed along the Rhine Valley in Germany and became part of the Palatine migration via Holland and England, finally settling at Red Hook in New York State. Early records show one Nicolaus Bohnenstiel taking up land at Lower Red Hook, Rhinebeck Colony, along the Hudson River. During the revolutionary war those who openly sided with England had their properties confiscated and, following the war, were ordered out of the country.

In 1784, Johan Bohnenstiel, who for some reason became John Bonisteel, accepted from the British Crown four hundred acres of land on a Lake Ontario bay called Kente, which for some reason became Quinte. John and his wife Catharine cleared away the forest, ploughed the land and planted his crops. For seven generations the process continued.

On my first trip to Germany in the late sixties, I didn't know the original spelling of the family name, and when I inquired about the root of Bonisteel, I was met with blank expressions. On later visits, as soon as I mentioned Bohnenstiel, I would be greeted with, "Oh yes ... that means bean stalk." This seemed to underscore my family's relationship with agricultural pursuits. Then there was the Irish connection ....

ST. PATRICK'S DAY

My grandmother's name was Kelly. I don't ever recall her influencing me much, but it must be that splash of Irish blood in my veins that starts me humming *"Too-ra-loo-ra-loo-ra"* whenever March 17th draws near.

There were three Kelly sisters: Clarissa, Emma and Marietta, known as Et – daughters of Reuben Kelly, an old pioneer of Sidney Township. Clarissa married my grandfather, a farmer. Emma and Et both married carpenters and they all lived within three miles of each other at Bayside, halfway between Trenton and Belleville. They died within nineteen months of each other in the early forties. All three were in their nineties.

It is Aunt Et I remember most. For many years she ran the grocery store and post office at Bayside and maintained a livery stable where the Toronto-Kingston stage stopped for fresh horses. When the bus and train became popular modes of transportation and rural mail delivery closed local post offices, Aunt Et went out of business at the age of ninety. She then came to live with us at our nearby farm and for the next six years was very much a part of my young life.

Perhaps it was from her I heard the Irish stories and legends of St. Patrick. It might have been she who introduced me to leprechauns and pots of gold at the ends of rainbows. I don't remember.

What I do remember is the music and the dancing at Riley's Pavilion. It was a large dance hall and community centre directly across from Aunt Et's store and post office. On Saturday nights when I was five or six, I would be packed up along with baskets of food and be taken to the dance. The men would sprinkle the floor with talcum powder, carry in wood for the huge pot-bellied stove and set up tables and chairs around the walls. The women piled the tables high with sandwiches, salads, cakes, pies and boilers full of hot coffee and tea.

The music was usually just a fiddle and a piano with someone "calling" for the square dances. One of the highlights for me was late in the evening when Riley himself, fortified no doubt by a drop of Irish elixir, took to the floor and did his remarkable clog dance.

This was not the jazzy, staccato tap dancing we know today but a fast-stepping, heel-and-toe routine performed with head and shoulders practically motionless and arms hanging straight down at his sides.

With the fiddle scraping out "Paddy's Reel" or "The Irish Washerwoman," we'd stand in a circle and clap in time until Riley finally collapsed in a chair from exhaustion or thirst.

It's all gone now. Riley's Pavilion was knocked down shortly after the post office closed to make way for the Number Two Highway that was required for Kingston-bound cars and trucks.

Our radios and TVs will serenade us this St. Patrick's day with "Danny Boy," "When Irish Eyes Are Smiling," and "MacNamara's Band." Our newspapers will report on a different Ireland.

I have been to Ireland only once. It was to do a television program on the conflict in and around Belfast.

The ugliness that I saw and filmed gave the lie to the generous, happy-go-lucky fun-loving Irish I had known as a boy. One late night in a secret IRA safe house I interviewed a woman with wispy white hair and a gentle face not unlike my dear Aunt Et. She told me about losing her husband in war and then a son and grandson to the bombings and street fighting. "My whole life has been full of fighting and killing," she said. "All I pray for now is love and peace to see me through my final days. But, mind you, there are a few people in high places I'd like to run a sword through right now."

I realized then that the Ireland of my fancy, the Emerald Isle of shamrocks, harps and the Blarney Stone was no more. And when I remembered the words to "Shan-von-voght," written in 1795, I decided it never had been.

> Oh Paddy dear, an' did ye
> hear the news that's going round?
> The shamrock is by law forbid
> to grow on Irish ground.
> No more St. Patrick's day we'll
> keep, his colour can't be seen.
> For they're hangin' men and women
> there for wearin' o' the green.

April

April

Aunt Et was ninety when I was six. When she moved to our farm, she brought a few things with her – some pictures and furniture, her bed and some blankets. She slept in the downstairs bedroom off the parlour so she wouldn't have to climb stairs. She needed someone to lean on when she walked, just to steady her so she wouldn't tip over. Tall, but bent, raw-boned and rather heavy, she always wore black taffeta dresses, high-buttoned boots and silk caps. She always called me Raymond.

"Why does she call me that? My name is Roy," I would shout angrily to my mother.

"Don't be upset. Remember she's very old and a little confused. Her son Raymond died after the First World War. She misses him very much. Does it really matter that much what she calls you?"

I got used to being called Raymond, having her lean on me when she wanted to walk around the house, hearing her sing old hymns alternately with music-hall tunes and generally having this ancient presence in my life.

In terms of being much of a help to the rest of the family in the fields, I was too young and Aunt Et was too old, so we sort of looked after each other.

"I think I see Clarissa coming across the field, Raymond. You'd better put the tea kettle on and get out some cake or cookies."

"There's no one coming, Aunt Et. I told you before that when you rock back and forth like that it makes the fence posts look as though they're moving."

"Don't argue with me, young man, just do what you're told."

So I would push the old enamel teapot to the front of the stove and hunt around in the pantry for Mom's cake or cookies and fill up a platter for our imaginary guest. By the time I was finished, Aunt Et would be sound asleep, snoring softly, often still rocking. Rather than see anything go to waste, I would have an afternoon snack.

It got so that whenever I felt hungry during the day I would go to Aunt Et and exclaim, "Say, isn't that Grandma coming across the fields?" It worked every time.

After supper she would insist on being pushed over to the sink where she would help do the dishes. Paying for her keep, she called it. A good number of dishes would slip from her trembling fingers and crack. She would also try to darn my socks or mittens in order to help out. My mother would have to take out her stitches and re-mend the holes, but no one ever suggested she stop doing her share. We knew how important it was for her to feel useful.

For the first few years she avidly read the daily paper with the aid of a magnifying glass and she also studied her Bible. Either her eyesight got worse or my grasp of the printed word got better because more and more she began asking me to read to her.

She would gently correct me when I stumbled over some confusing biblical verse and catch me up short when I tried to skip over the boring bits.

"Now, Raymond, remember every word in the Bible is the word of God and must be read the way it was written. You've completely missed the dimensions of the holy city of Jerusalem with its twelve gates where nothing unclean shall enter and the streets are of pure gold as translucent glass." Oh well!

She would join the family around the battery radio as we listened to the news from Europe in those early war years. One night, as two commentators reported on the activities of Generals Montgomery and McNaughton, we heard Aunt Et speculate as to when Sherman would be making his move. Her mind had slipped back to another war. I checked some dates in my history book and discovered that, yes indeed, she had been in her mid-twenties when Lincoln was president.

As the years went by, her eyesight and hearing disintegrated, but I don't ever recall her having a sick day. Her mind flitted in and out of reality, but this made us perfect for each other. At that age my mind was somewhere else most of the time.

Thinking I was her son Raymond, she naturally assumed I would be taking over the store and post office, and so insisted on helping me with my numbers and my attitude. This pleased my parents since I certainly needed the assistance. I learned my times tables, long division and percentages as I learned manners, civility and courtesy in preparation for a non-existent job.

In the fall of 1942 when I was twelve and Aunt Et was ninety-six, it was silo-filling time at our farm and the neighbour men were coming in from the fields for supper. I ran ahead into the house to tell my mother the men were arriving. Aunt Et said she would like to lie down for a brief nap before eating. We helped her into the bedroom where she stretched out, folded her hands over her chest and went to sleep. She never woke up.

With the exception of Aunt Et, no one in our family got very excited over religion. I think everyone believed in God and certainly my Mother embraced all the Christian virtues, but it was never a central part of our life. Mum was a member of the Women's Institute and the Ladies' Aid and my brothers and sisters joined the Young People's Union but they did this not so much out of commitment to a cause as for social reasons.

My mother enjoyed reciting. She had a good voice and a fine stage presence. Whether at a large church gathering or a small sewing circle, she was inevitably called upon to perform. I still have yellowed newspaper clippings that proclaim "Florence Bonisteel did several selections from Shakespeare, Burns and Kipling, concluding with her stirring account of the 'Ride of Jenny MacNeil.'"

My brother Bert was a fine harmonica player and was often part of a congregation social. I don't recall ever seeing my father in church but I recently came across his old farm journal with the entry "Minister came by today. Gave him two dollars."

This doesn't seem like much until you note the date. In the summer of 1930, that was two days' pay.

One of my earliest memories of church was going with my mother, whose maiden name had been Hunt, and her sister-in-law Helen. One Sunday Aunt Helen found a change purse with money in it on the floor under the pew. She wrote a note and put it on the offering plate as it passed by. When the minister received the collection, he opened the note and announced, "There has been a small, black purse found this morning. The owner can go to Helen Hunt for it." The idea of the minister telling someone to go to Hell broke up the congregation. This same minister had a strange way of ending every sermon and I can still recall trying desperately not to laugh at his concluding remarks. He would remove his spectacles, lean over the pulpit and solemnly intone, "Now remember. Fight on. Struggle on. Stick it out and see what the end looks like. Amen."

My memories of early religion are generally centred around the holidays of which I was very fond.

EASTER

This year Easter falls on April 19th. Last year it was March 30th. Next year this time we'll be in the middle of the Easter weekend. This moveable feast of baked ham and chocolate eggs hops around spring like the Easter bunny itself.

Here's how to figure out when to buy your new bonnet. Easter is always the first Sunday after the full moon, on, or next after, the vernal equinox, which is March 21st. If the full moon falls on a Sunday, Easter is observed one week later. That is, unless you subscribe to the Eastern Orthodox method of calculating Passover, which could push Easter well into May.

Since most of us are not proficient with sextant or slide rule and are not on the mailing list of the patriarch of Alexandria, we have to rely on the calendar makers and the *Farmer's Almanac*.

When I was a boy, Easter was the only time I was required to go to church. Many errant families still make this once-yearly pilgrimage.

A minister friend of mine always concludes the Easter message to his overflowing congregation by saying, "Since I won't see many of you again until this time next year, I'd like to take the opportunity to wish you a Merry Christmas."

My family went to White's Church on the Number Two Highway at Bayside. It was the first church built in Sidney Township. The land was donated and the lumber for its construction sawed by United Empire Loyalist pioneer Reuben White in

1836. For reasons I never understood, they knocked the church down and sold the land in 1968. I can't speak for the other fifty-one weeks of the year, but at Easter it was a very special place to be.

Festooned with lilies, geraniums and potted palms, the church looked and smelled like an arboretum.

The minister's sermon contained all the ingredients of a thrilling adventure story. An innocent man is captured and dragged before the governor, stripped, beaten and taunted. He's nailed to a cross and stabbed while soldiers roll dice for his clothes. Then a real boffo ending – he comes to life again and walks out of his tomb to the amazement of both his captors and colleagues.

Long before Fulton Oursler wrote his book, I realized this was "The Greatest Story Ever Told." And the singing, so upbeat and triumphant.

> Jesus Christ is risen today-ay
> Helllll-lay-loo-oo-yuh.

No mumbling over obscure, draggy lyrics. Even if you didn't know all the words to all the verses, you could shout that last line with the best in the choir and the congregation.

The rest of the day paled in comparison ... at least at our house. We listened to the radio for the fashion parades being described from Fifth Avenue in New York and the Boardwalk in Atlantic City. We could crank up the phonograph and play Irving Berlin's new hit, which contained my favourite rhyming couplet: "You'll find that you're / In the rotogravure."

But mainly I remember trying to see how many eggs we could eat. It was a competition among my brothers and sisters. Platters of fried eggs at breakfast, devilled with mustard and paprika for lunch and boiled for supper. Each meal on Easter day was a scene from *Cool Hand Luke*. It wasn't until many years later I realized this was in lieu of candy which we simply couldn't afford. On the farm, eggs were always in plentiful supply. By the time I heard there was an Easter bunny that was supposed to come around and distribute chocolate eggs and jelly beans, I was too old to be interested.

I was in Nairobi in 1975 reporting on the meeting of the World Council of Churches when the subject of Easter was brought before the assembly. From the press room in the grandly ostentatious Kenyatta Centre, media representatives from all over the globe watched as the delegates voted to set the day for Easter, once and for all, on the second Sunday of April. When the vote passed, there was a whoop of joy from the clergy.

Alas, the euphoria faded in the following years. The vote could only constitute a recommendation and the proposal didn't go over well with the members back home who some-how thought their leaders were blas-phemously tampering with a sacred rule.

The mind-boggling calculations are actually based on establishing the day for the old pagan festival cele-brating the spring goddess Eostre. With that in mind, perhaps it's time we stop hopscotching all over the calendar and pin down a permanent day we could remember from year to year. I'm sure many would respond …"Helllll-lay-loo-oo-yuh."

Planning events according to cycles of the moon was not unknown in our farming community. As a matter of fact, great care was taken by some to see that animals were bred and crops were sown at the most propitious lunar time.

My father pretended to pay scant attention to this practice but often, when our bull had been observed mounting one of the cows in the pasture, I would notice Dad hurry into the house, check the wall calendar, which listed the moon's phases, then make a pencilled entry in his farm diary.

For many farmers in our area the moon was regarded as female and related closely to fertility. The weaning of both pigs and calves from the mother was always scheduled to take place during the last quarter and certainly before an eclipse.

It was thought that when the moon was between new and first quarter it was the ideal time to plant or transplant above-ground crops such as strawberries, corn or leafy vegetables. Potatoes, carrots, turnips and other below-ground produce should be planted when the moon was between full and last quarter. When the moon was between last quarter and new, no planting was undertaken. This was the time to destroy weeds, burn brush, get rid of pests, cultivate or plough.

I'm not sure if the land was any more fruitful as a result of our following these astrological guidelines, but I feel it gave us an almost spiritual relationship with the earth, our animals and our environment.

RENEWAL

A radio producer from Regina called recently to ask if I would take part in a special Easter program being prepared for broadcast. She had come up with an intriguing approach to a problem that has bedevilled broadcasters and journalists for years. How do you satisfy the need, some would call it an obsession, to say something fresh and innovative about a story that's been around for a couple of thousand years?

This producer came up with the idea of tieing the Easter story in with concern for the environment. Perhaps this holy season could provide inspiration for re-examining attitudes about our natural resources and the preservation of our ecological system.

I thought she had a good premise and since I care about the future of our world, I agreed to take part. The interview went roughly like this:

Q. What are your earliest memories of any form of conservation?

A. I was born into a farm family. Farmers in those days practised conservation to survive. For example our woodlot was the only source of lumber for building, fuel for the home and sap for maple syrup. I was taught how to tap trees in a non-damaging way. Old wood was cleaned out to make room for young growth and new trees were planted when one was cut down. Crop rotation was practised to eliminate herbicides and fence rows were allowed to stand to prevent erosion and give shelter to birds and small animals.

Q. When did your fears for the environment begin?

A. When I was in my twenties I worked at a radio station in the Niagara district and saw first-hand the acres of precious orchard land being dug up for subdivisions and paved over for parking lots. There are only two areas of Canada where tender fruits such as peaches, grapes, nectarines and apricots can grow and both the Niagara Peninsula and the Okanagan Valley are systematically being destroyed.

Q. Are you personally involved in helping conserve areas of this country?

A. Yes, two in particular. The Temagami region, north of Sudbury and North Bay, Ontario, is unique in the world for its 400-year-old red and white pine, its 3,000-year-old aboriginal trails and the world's only source of nearly extinct aurora trout. The Stein River Valley, B.C.'s largest chunk of untouched wilderness, is over 44,000 acres of thick evergreens in the south-west of that province and has become an environmental war zone. The Lytton and Mount Currie Indian bands call the land their "spiritual food." In these two areas mismanagement by both government and industry must be stopped before both are lost.

Q. Why should we bring these concerns to people at this time of year?

A. Because Easter means renewal and beginning again. It also means confession for past sins and redemption to allow a new start. I'm not a theologian but it seems to me the idea of new life for our endangered land or a cleaning-up of the atmosphere are very religious things to consider.

Q. The Book of Genesis says man was given dominion over the world and everything in it by God. Was Genesis wrong?

A. The interpretation is wrong. It says that God looked at the newly created world and declared it was good. All living things were in balance with one another. We were given the chance to tend the world and be stewards of this creation, not to reduce it to a pile of polluted garbage.

Q. We are told that the cost of reversing present environmental conditions would be 150 billion dollars a year. Can we afford it?

A. Considering that is only one-sixth of the annual 900 billion dollars spent on armaments it's a case of setting our priorities.

Q. Any other thoughts about Easter?

A. Just that the night before He was crucified Jesus chose to spend time in a garden. He drew apart in this wilderness area to pray and meditate. It might be a good thought for Easter to pledge ourselves to create and maintain more quiet garden spots before it's too late.

Announcer: Thanks for being a part of our program and Happy Easter.

My father's love of the land, his concern for animal life and his determination always to do the right thing are what I remember most about him.

He found it difficult to express tender emotions toward people. I never remember sitting on his lap or being kissed or cuddled by him, yet I have seen him search through half a winter's night for a stray calf, then hold it in his arms until morning to make sure it survived.

My mother called him Benson, neighbours called him Ben. Only a few close friends called him Benny. My brothers and sisters called him Pa, some of them behind his back spoke of "the old man." I opted for Dad.

He never hit or spanked his children to enforce discipline. He didn't have to. A steely, penetrating gaze from his pale blue eyes would have you jumping to obey or confessing any number of misdemeanours. He was fair, honest and, looking back now, one of the bravest men I ever knew. But at one time I mistook bravery for stupidity.

One of my earliest memories was of a cold winter night when I was about four years old. My job was to carry the lantern while Dad gave the final day's ration of hay and grain to the animals. It was hard following his footsteps through the snow, but I managed to catch up with him just as he opened the large barn doors to reveal the dark stable, steamy with the breath of the cloistered livestock. As the lantern glow flooded over the barn's interior, it caught the glint of two fierce eyes in a corner near the mangers. A skunk was crouched over a nest of newly smashed eggs that, even in that dim illumination, showed the remains of unborn chicks.

You don't have to live on a farm to know that you always give a skunk a wide berth. Even a four-year-old boy knows it's stupid to get too near. While I froze in indecision, my father continued his rapid stride across the barn floor. He reached down, grabbed the skunk by its white-streaked back, turned and hurled it out through the open doors. It sailed up and over the manure pile and landed in a snowbank as shocked and helpless with surprise as I was.

I guess I should have realized then that a man who would pick up a skunk and toss it had very little fear of anything.

When I was twelve, I was assigned to driving

our team of horses during harvest time, when the sheaves of grain were loaded onto the wagon for the trip to the threshing machine at the barn. We were on a neighbour's place and farmers from miles around had come to help out, as was the custom in this annual ritual. As I drove from stook to stook up a rather steep knoll, my father placed the sheaves on the wagon, alternating head and stalk and carefully tramping them into rows, so the load would be stable. On another wagon, half the field away, was a man whose heavy load was lurching and swaying as his exhausted horses struggled to climb the incline.

His team bore the signs of ill use. Their ribs clearly showed beneath hide lathered in sweat. Using the lines as a whip, he lashed them repeatedly and cursed their faltering attempts to move forward.

"Come with me," my father said. I wrapped our own team's lines securely to the hayrack and we both jumped to the ground. Even at twelve, I still had to trot to keep up with his long-legged pace heading toward the other wagon.

As we got near, I saw with dismay the man grab his long-tined pitchfork and jab one of the struggling horses in the rump. My father leaped between the horses and the wagon and deliberately unhitched the team.

"Take them to the barn," he told me. "Give them water and grain. I'll see to them later."

As I turned to go, I saw him fix the astonished farmer with that gaze I knew so well and watched the man and his abandoned wagon full of grain roll slowly back down the hill. The incident was never mentioned again.

Dad's actions were consistent with his refusal to allow things to happen that he didn't consider right. I finally came to the conclusion that my father knew no fear. What, in my young mind, was a stupid thing to do was for him simply seeing that the right thing was done.

Proof came one day when I was twenty. By this time, I was a reporter on the *Courier-Advocate*, a bi-weekly newspaper in Trenton. Since I was the paper's only news reporter and was on duty at irregular hours, I chose to live in town instead of with my parents on the farm.

Saturday afternoons my father would come into town for supplies, as did most farmers in the area, and after requisite trips to the grist mill, hardware store or barber shop, he would stop in at the Gilbert House for a few draught beers. Wanting to get caught up on the home news of the week, I would join him and spend a couple of pleasant hours sipping and chatting in a quiet corner of the bar. I was actually a year under the drinking age, but by this time I was as tall as Dad, about six-foot-two, and no one questioned me.

One April afternoon, right in the middle of a story about the lower forty being flooded with the spring run-off, I looked over Dad's shoulder and saw to my dismay "Terrible Turk" come through the half-doors and commandeer a table. He was unknown to Dad but there were few people in town who hadn't been harassed or at least intimidated by this ex-boxer whose real name was Harold Turkoff.

I had recently covered two trials in a local county courtroom where he had been charged with

DESERONTO PUBLIC LIBRARY

both aggravated assault and break and enter. After his acquittal on both charges, when witnesses refused to testify, he bragged to me and several others that no one would dare convict him for fear of "having their brains punched out."

The waiters visibly cringed as Turk slammed the top of the table and shouted for "half a dozen cold ones." It was a liquor licensing board law in those days that only two beers per patron be placed on a table at one time, but laws meant nothing to Terrible Turk. A waiter rushed to obey, then hurried back to the bar without waiting for payment. There was a very good possibility there would be none.

I found myself only half listening to Dad as he continued talking about new fencing that would have to be built around the flooded area to keep the cows out. My eyes were on Turk who began to stack his quickly emptied beer glasses pyramid-fashion on the table, yelling obscenities at everyone in proximity. With a sweep of his arm, he sent the glasses crashing to the floor. Other customers ceased talking. Some began to tiptoe out.

Frustrated by the continuous interruption, Dad finally turned to locate the source of the racket. Then, to my horror, he began to rise from his chair. "Dad," I whispered, "Don't be stupid. The guy's crazy."

My father got to his feet and started walking in the direction of Turk's table. I noticed for the first time how old he seemed. By now, he was in his sixties. He looked tired and his back was becoming thin and stooped. His once purposeful stride was slower and more deliberate. As he reached the table, he placed his hand on Turk's massive shoulder and I thought, "Please, God … no."

Turk turned and I could see the glower on his face as his eyes travelled up my father's tall frame. His gaze stopped when it reached my father's eyes. I couldn't see Dad's face but I heard him say, "You're making too much noise. I'm trying to visit with my son. Either keep quiet or get out. And, be sure to pay for the broken glasses."

The bar was hushed. Turk slowly rose. Even at full height, he barely came up to the bib on my father's overalls. For a moment they stood looking at each other. Then, without checking the amount, Turk laid a few crumpled bills on the table, turned and walked out through the doors.

Dad returned to our table, sat down and continued describing the new fence that would be built with leftover rails, since it would only be temporary. He didn't even pause when a waiter sat two glasses of beer on the table and said gratefully, "These are on the house."

My father lived to be eighty-seven. Although retired from the farm and frail with the ravages of age, his last years were spent growing vegetables and shrubs in a small garden just for the pleasure of watching the cycle of nature unfold and feeling the rich earth in his hands. I remember, in his final days, how gaunt and feeble his body had become, but how his eyes remained as bright and piercing as ever.

In my mind's eye I picture him, mostly in the spring, chafing with the restlessness that comes to a house-bound outdoorsman. At the first scent of warm air, I see him striding over the land as if willing the earth to thaw by his very presence.

THE PROMISE OF SPRING

The poet proclaims, "Oh to be in England now that April's there." The song writer extolls, "April in Paris, chestnuts in blossom." I've been in both places during this month but still prefer the Bay of Quinte area.

To appreciate spring, you have to endure winter. April cannot be the spirited life-giving month it is, if you haven't experienced the sleet, snow and sub-zero temperatures of preceding months. As the ice melts and the air warms, our local corner of the universe awakes and we feel closer than any other time of year to the rhythms of nature.

To a boy on the farm, April meant switching from our heavy winter Mackinaw rubbers to those slip-on gumboots with the red band around the tops that gauged how deep you could wade in the creek or pond. An old-fashioned game of chicken was played with other kids by tempting fate as you stepped farther and farther into the stream, feeling the strong pull of the current against your legs and watching the water rise closer to the red band. When a slip of the foot or a spongy part of the creek bed sent an icy torrent into your boot, you screamed aloud, lost the game and squished your way home.

Meteorologists now confirm my contention that the winter snow was deeper and the spring run-off heavier when I was a boy. They finally give credence to a father whose children always looked askance when he talked of the "good old days."

The April creek overflowed the culverts on the second concession, coursed through our farm, flooded White's sideroad and cascaded into the bay. Pike, mudcats and suckers frolicked in the cold, fresh water that filled the swamps and marshlands. Here on spring afternoons and evenings neighbours with three-pronged spears harvested many a tasty fish fry. Spearing was illegal, but the game warden looked the other way when a farmer caught only for his own use and on his own property.

This April, the same creek bears no resemblance to its former majesty. It is narrow and shallow from the melting of a skimpy snowfall. Sub-divisions and their septic tanks have drained off its force and changed its directions. An expanded air base rerouted its entry into the Bay of

DESERONTO PUBLIC LIBRARY

Quinte and seepage from a closed township dump has turned its water putrid. The odd fish makes its way languidly up as far as the sideroad unthreatened by spear or hook. No one of sane mind would eat it.

The struggle between nature's death and rebirth has marked April as a month of paradox for philosophers and poets. Canada's brilliant Marshall McLuhan died in 1980, a victim of a massive stroke. For some time following the attack, he was only able to repeat single words or lines of memorized poetry. His daughter remembers that in his final spring, looking out the window at the rain, he recited lines from "The Wasteland" by T.S. Eliot, beginning, "April is the cruelest month."

Unguarded by snow and not yet decorated by grass or flowers, this month is laid bare. At least in Canada, we are brought face to face with April's ambiguities. The ravages of the past winter, like the neglect of past years, are there for all to see. The promise of spring, like the hope for a new environmental consciousness, is all around us. A memory of something fine means little unless others can experience it too. I have had the thrill of wading in the clear,

swollen creeks of April. My grandchildren deserve no less.

May

May

I never minded being the youngest of ten kids even though there were some obvious drawbacks. You seldom got new clothes since there were plenty of hand-me-downs to choose from; your opinion didn't count in any decision-making; and you were generally ignored by everyone because they were all older than you and therefore smarter.

The good part was that no one really expected much of you. You were fairly well left to your own devices and as long as you stayed out of the way and kept reasonably quiet, life was just fine.

The sibling next to me was my sister Flossie, seven years older. When I was starting grade one, she was in grade eight, so for most of my primary school life there was no family member to interfere. This meant that my progress in class, my relations with fellow students or the teacher were never subjects for family discussion. With so much going on at home on the farm, they were hardly aware of my leaving in the morning or returning at night.

I was alone a lot but I don't remember ever being lonely. In the schizophrenic way of children, I led many lives. Over the miles I walked daily to and from school, I was a Gene Autry cowboy herding the bewildered cows into the far corners of the back pasture; I was a Tarzan swinging from the trees in the sugar bush, scaring the squirrels with my famous ape-man yell; I was a dashing Tyrone Power pirate leaping from the crooked-rail-fence clipper ship that surrounded our fields.

Education in the one-room schools of the thirties was a hit-and-miss situation. It depended a great deal on the teacher and since you sometimes had the same one for all eight grades, you were stuck with what you got. The one I had for the first seven years had very little education herself and bolstered what few gifts she had with liberal applications of her thick leather strap. The last time she strapped me was in the spring of grade six. I had unwisely pointed out her mispronunciation of a word she had written on the blackboard. This was not the first time I had corrected her, but I think she was determined it would be the last.

I recognized the look of fury in her eyes and knew what was coming when she yanked open her desk drawer. The familiar hush fell over the school as she headed toward me. What the hell, I thought, I might as well go for broke. "By the way," I said evenly, "you also misspelled the word."

When I returned in the fall to begin grade seven, my nemesis was visibly shaken when she saw I had grown about six inches during the summer and was an unlikely candidate for her bullying. From then on, when she wrote a word of more than two syllables on the board, she either looked it up in the dictionary in advance or glanced over to me for a nod of approval afterwards. I was glad a new teacher was hired for my final year of public school.

THE MONTH OF FIRSTS

Modern May doesn't seem to have the romantic traditions I remember as a boy. It was a month of firsts. Without fear of frost you could safely set out those first garden plants tenderly started on the windowsill. It was the first time you permanently removed your long underwear, which was the exciting prelude to the first skinny dip of the year.

And whatever happened to Arbor Day? It was started in 1872 by a future U.S. secretary of agriculture as a day in the spring for communities to plant trees. I'm not sure our local board of education knew this when I went to school or perhaps they just saw a better use for child labour. We were told it was a day to clean up the school yard. Armed with rakes and sickles borrowed from home, we chopped down weed stalks, piled up dead leaves and collected the debris of winter into one big pile in the corner of the yard. Since we had only about twenty kids in our local one-roomer, it took most of the day to tidy up the full acre lot. In the late afternoon, our teacher would strike a match to start a bonfire and we were allowed to sit on the damp ground and sing patriotic songs.

In May of 1940 our teacher announced we were going to start a Victory Garden. Apparently growing your own vegetables was a way to help the war effort. This might have made sense for people living in cities but at old School Section Number Four all of us were farm kids and we had acres of vegetables at home. We certainly didn't need to be taught hoeing. It was right up there with walking and milking cows – one of the first things we learned in life. Of course we wanted to do our bit to defeat Hitler, so we dug up a fifty-foot square corner of the school yard, divided it into plots with binder twine, stuck in the seeds and patiently waited for the war to end.

Since the school year ended first and there was no one around during July and August to water our Victory Garden, the plants shrivelled up and it was left to next Arbor Day to clean up the mess. Its failure, however, resulted in a new project the next year, learning how to knit. Our teacher decided we should make an afghan to send to our soldiers. We unravelled old sweaters and toques our families didn't need anymore and knitted eight-by-ten-inch squares, which were then sewn into a piebald quilt for shipment overseas. Whether or not our masterpieces ever found their way to a foxhole I'll never know, but knitting was one of the few skills I learned in school that I never forgot. Today I can still "knit one, purl two" with the best of them.

Meanwhile, back to the old swimming hole. We had two of them. There was the quarry on Aiken's side-road and the sand-pit on White's side-road. Both excavations were the result of the large amount of gravel and sand needed to build the Trenton Air Base in the late twenties and early thirties. The quarry was a deep rock-faced chasm that had been abandoned when an underground spring filled it with water. It had no bottom! At least that's what my older brothers said when I was young and dumb enough to believe every scary thing they told me. What a triumphant day it was when I finally learned to dog-paddle across its vast forty-foot length, conquering the fear of sinking forever or at best surfacing in China.

The sand-pit, on the other hand,

was seldom more than shoulder-blade deep and was merely water collected from winter snows and early spring rain. May 24th was the time for the long-awaited first dip, though sometimes there was a skimming of ice over its surface. For some of the boys this was also the first complete bath of the year, so cakes of Ivory or Sunlight were brought in and gave the sand-pit the appearance of one large communal tub.

It could also be scary. When the other boys were there splashing and thrashing about, it was OK, but sometimes on hot summer afternoons a solitary swim would find you sharing your rural paradise with water snakes and snapping turtles. In the thirties and forties the greatest fear was instilled by our parents as polio claimed more and more victims. We called it infantile paralysis and as the days grew hotter and the sand-pit developed a greenish tinge we were banned from its shallow depths. The snakes, turtles and mosquitoes had it all to themselves.

Today with in-ground cement pools, above-ground vinyl pools and especially indoor health spa pools, that first spring dip loses its enchantment.

Our lakes and rivers are more contaminated than the old sand-pit ever was and we are forced to swim red-eyed through filtered water doused with chlorine and muriatic acid. In most places bathing suits are required.

Shakespeare spoke of "May's new-fangled mirth." Surely that was tossing all your clothes on a fence and leaping into a chilly spring pond.

A few years ago, after I had spoken to a convention in Vancouver, a woman about my age came up to me and said that she too had been born in the Bay of Quinte area and had lived on "the front" of Sidney Township. She wondered if the old sand-pit was still there.

"How did you know about that?" I asked, thinking it was only a part of life for "me and the boys."

She replied, "We girls always went back there and hid in the sumac bushes to watch the boys swimming naked. For us it was sort of a spring tradition."

There is one spring tradition that is never enjoyed by young people across this land, whether they live in the country or the city. Some sadistic person or group a long time ago decided that the only way to tell whether you had any brains or not was to devise tests. I have never seen any correlation between the results of school examinations and a person's intelligence or life achievements. The only difference these days from when I went to school is the language used in educational assessments. The trauma remains the same.

THE END OF SCHOOL

'Tis the season of exams. Normally bright and clear-eyed youths are walking our streets with distracted minds and glazed stares as "finals" from kindergarten to Ph.D. assert their rites of spring. Homework is being pursued with new vigour and textbooks, uncracked since September, are seeing the light of midnight cramming as the days before exam week dwindle down to a precious few.

I don't understand the examination process anymore. Apparently there is nothing final about it. You can continue by dropping subjects you don't pass, change courses in midstream, finish assignments at some later date and generally hold your head high no matter what's in it.

My job takes me into quite a few classrooms from time to time and I rub shoulders at conventions and education seminars with hundreds of teachers and professors each year, but I seem to have a learning disability when it comes to the language of academe. It's the acronyms I find most confusing.

A teacher friend of mine related a conversation apparently typical in modern education. She was new to teaching, had learned many of the catchphrases at teacher's college but was not prepared for what greeted her in the staff lounge.

Teacher A: Do you think they'll reduce the magic number in the next contract?

Teacher B: I think it's more important to reduce the STR particularly with the new OSIS programs. By the way did Fred get his senior social science? I know he wants to get his OSAP forms in as soon as possible.

Teacher C: Did you read this? "Norm referenced evaluation criticized in light of GPA system." I didn't know the OSSTF was heading in that direction.

Teacher A: I still like the old bell curve. It helps you skew in the right direction.

Translation: The magic number refers to years of service plus age, allowing a teacher to retire. STR is the student-teacher ratio in the classroom. OSIS is the program that replaced grade thirteen in Ontario.OSIS requires students to get credits in specified categories at both the junior and senior levels. OSAP is sometimes referred to as the Ontario Stereo Aquisition Program, but is the students' assistance program. Norm referenced evaluation looks at a specific class and judges the student accordingly, as opposed to using objective criteria. GPA means grade point average, out of a possible total of four. The bell curve is an outmoded way of lowering or raising class marks based on overall averages. Skew is the total number of As, Bs and Cs deemed appropriate to a given class.

There was a time when educational levels were simply called public school, high school and university. There was no pre-kindergarten, kindergarten, junior high or community college. When you successfully passed all your subjects at one level, you moved on to the next. You had to achieve at least 51 percent in every subject. If you failed one, you took the entire year over again.

To get from public school to high school, you tried what were called "entrance exams." For me and my fellow rural one-roomers, it meant showing up at the Belleville Collegiate and Vocational School where, on the appropriate days and under the watchful eye of a senior teacher, we wrote our "finals."

Most of us bicycled into the city early in the morning in order to be in our seats before nine o'clock. The exam papers were distributed face down on our desks and at exactly nine we were told, "Turn them over and begin ... NOW." Three hours in the morning and three in the afternoon for two days would cover all the subjects.

In order for me to be on time, and as a special treat, my father had loaned me his new pocket watch for the occasion. It was a unique model in that it had no hands. The time appeared in little squares on the clock face much like a mileage counter in a car. I found it so intriguing that several times that first morning I took it out to sneak a peek and watch the seconds and minutes roll up.

"What are you holding under your desk, young man?" boomed the teacher.

"I was just looking at my watch, sir," I replied, startled.

"We'll see about this!"

He made me stand and empty my pockets. He searched my sleeves and arms for illicit inscriptions and then, grudgingly convinced I wasn't cheating, confiscated my dad's watch. I had to ask him for it back when the whole process was finished the next day.

You never found out your results until they were printed in the local newspaper some time in July complete with your name and percentages. I can't remember how I did, but I must have squeaked through because I received my PHL. That's Passport to Higher Learning.

I left school each spring with very mixed feelings. First there was a sense of freedom, a release from the tedium of Geography at 11:00 and English at 1:00, day in and day out. But ahead was the routine of farm life, much more taxing to the body, but hardly a challenge to the brain. That is not to say we were without inventiveness. Country life meant using what was at hand, fixing what was broken again and again, leaving nothing to waste.

RECYCLING

There are many blessings enjoyed by rural dwellers. The changing seasons, fresh air, space and a feeling of being in tune with nature. In recent years we would likely add to this list regular garbage collections. It would be difficult to imagine what we would do without it. Yet I recall a time when not only was there no garbage pickup, there was no garbage.

Long before "biodegradable" and "recycling" became such common words in our modern language, both were happening as a matter of course in our daily living habits. Those of us who lived in a less affluent time saw little waste. When the axiom "a penny saved is a penny earned" was part of our childhood understanding of life, nothing was discarded. Especially for those of us who grew up in farming areas, everything was used.

Milk, for example, came straight from the cow to the table. No plastic jugs, bags or cartons. The garden and orchard provided fresh fruit and vegetables in season and our winter supplies were canned in glass mason jars that had been handed down for generations. Our own animals were the source of the family's meat, usually processed in the fall and frozen or cured for winter use.

Table scraps were fed to the house pets. If they desired more exotic fare, there were always plenty of mice around for the cats and the odd woodchuck for the dogs. I'm sure modern veterinarians would frown at this diet, but I doubt if it was much worse than what you see when you open a can today of something called Luxury Pussy Din-Din. There were very few cans of any kind that entered the home. The ones that did were cleaned and used to store things like nails, bolts, pins or buttons.

Clothes were passed down from parents to children and from one sibling to the next. Holes and rips were patched and mended. Has anyone darned a sock in the last twenty-five years?

Apparel of all kinds eventually ended up in a rag bag where much of it was sewn into home-made blankets called crazy quilts. It was somewhat comforting just before dozing off at night to look at your coverlet and see recognizable scraps of material from your family's favourite clothing.

Newspapers, magazines and catalogues had two very important functions. One was to start the morning fires in the wood stoves throughout the house and the other was to stock the outdoor privy. Only the highest quality publications went there. Potato peelings, lettuce leaves and any other residue from meal preparation went as a treat for the pigs or on the garden compost heap.

I find it interesting how little we've learned over the years. When we delivered our milk to the local cheese factory each day, we would refill our forty-gallon cans with whey left over from the previous day's production. This, mixed with ground grains, formed the basis of the pig's feeding program. Two years ago the United States Department of Agriculture, concerned about the large amount of whey that dairies and cheese factories were dumping into streams, launched a $200,000 research project. Guess what? They found that it could be recycled as nutritious feed for farm animals. Farmers in the Quinte area could have told them that for free.

No one really wants to go back to the old wood-chopping, water-hauling days of yesteryear. Advances in science and technology have provided us with an abundant and enjoyable life-style. But we have also developed a throw-away mentality that has buried us in mountains of garbage and a sea of pollution. Perhaps what we should recycle are the old-fashioned ethics of thrift, prudence and common sense.

June

June

I suppose we were poor. There was certainly no money around, yet I never felt poor. Most everyone I saw looked the same as I did. All the boys at school wore bib overalls, flannelette shirts, wool socks and black leather work boots. The girls wore dresses or pleated skirts with sweaters. Everything we wore was patched, darned or resoled. All of our fathers were farmers who raised dairy cattle that provided the milk for the local cheese factory. All of our mothers baked bread, rendered lard and kept a few hens for "egg money."

Any extra money went into the farm for better stock or more reliable machinery. Families helped each other, not just for threshing, silo-filling or barn-raising but in times of illness or at birth and death. In a sense, our poverty bound us together.

You did what you could to make an extra dollar. We would cut extra firewood in the winter to sell in town the following year. One or two of my brothers would spend a day working at the air base with a team of our horses for some added income. The pay, as I remember, was seventy-five cents per man and one dollar for the team. If an animal died or was slaughtered for meat, the hide brought a few dollars at the Trenton tannery.

We were fortunate in being one of the few farms in the area with purebred breeding stock. We had a registered Percheron stud named Gilbert, a purebred Holstein-Friesian bull named Petigie Ragapple II and a Tamworth hog whose name I forget but who was a tireless performer when the occasion demanded. Neighbouring farmers who wanted to upgrade their livestock would bring their female animals at the appropriate time to our place for servicing. As the youngest, I was usually the only one not out in the fields working and so was often available to oversee the job and collect the money. We charged five dollars for Gilbert, three dollars for P.R. II and two dollars for the hog.

The story is told that one day when I was five years old I answered our door to a neighbouring farmer who asked to speak to my father. I told him my father was back in the woods working but I could look after things and I knew the rates.

"Well, it's not about that," he said. "It's about your brother Frank. He's been spending a lot of time with my daughter and I think it's getting serious."

"In that case you'll have to talk to my father," I'm reputed to have said. "I don't know how much he charges for Frank."

HAYING

More poems and songs have been written about June than any other month, and no wonder! As James

Lowell said, "Then, if ever, come perfect days." Farmers certainly hope so because June is haying month.

You can rhapsodize and warble about the "scent of new-mown hay," but unless you take to the back roads this month, roll down the car window and inhale, you'll miss the exquisite perfume of swathed alfalfa, timothy, red or white clover.

Haying in Canada has gone through an astounding progression in the last fifty years. Our forefathers cut it with scythes, stacked it with wooden forks and stuffed it into makeshift mows to provide winter fodder for the horses and cattle.

In my lifetime the changes have been remarkable.

First the hay was cut with a horse-drawn mower, its sharp pointed knives scissoring the stalks into flat layers while rabbits and mice scampered to safety in the tree lines. Then the curvy-tongued hay rake gathered it into long windrows where it was piled with pitchforks into "cocks" about every ten feet.

The earliest method of unloading I remember was with the iron hayfork, a wishbone-shaped instrument that speared the hay from a loaded wagon and, through a series of rope cables and pulleys, hauled it into the two mows on either side of the barn. It took about eight tries and as many people to unload the wagon.

Then came slings. These were rope affairs that were placed on the bottom, in the centre and near the top of the wagon as the load was built in the field. Using the same pulley technique at the barn, one-third of the load was completly lifted into the mows at one time.

Building a proper load of hay was a science only older and experienced farmers could handle. The first fork-fuls were placed on the right hand corner of the wagon continuing down and around the sides. Then the centre of the wagon was filled and tramped, thereby tieing in the hay to prevent shifting and sliding. This process continued until the load extended high above the racks and everyone involved was helped aboard for the ride to the barn.

As the loose hay was dumped into the mows, it was spread, tramped and sprinkled with buckets of coarse salt to prevent heating that could cause spontaneous combustion.

Improper care at this stage resulted in many a fall barn-burning. The salt also added a perk to the palates of pasture-hungry cows and horses during the winter.

The invention of the hay loader, a large conveyer with claws that scooped the hay from the windrows and tossed it on the back of the wagon, saved a lot of work and cut down on the number of people needed in the field.

But the big advance came with the baler. First using wire, then twine, this remarkable machine packaged the hay into neat rectangular blocks and newer models actually put the bales on the wagon. The hay could now be cut, cured and baled at the peak of its June perfection, then stacked squarely and efficiently in the barn.

The latest in hay technology produces those huge, round coils that you see lying in long mountains near the barns as you drive through the country these days.

Theoretically a farmer never has to touch the hay anymore. Fork-lifts and front-end loaders do the lifting and hauling. There is no need for the hay mow any longer. When one of these monsters is uncoiled in the yard, animals can munch for days. The outside may get somewhat soggy and weather-beaten if not covered, but, as some farmers say, "What's a little waste in the name of efficiency?"

Yet, for me, those hay mows inside the barn were special places on a farm. They were the recreation room, the gymnasium and the meeting place for farm kids.

Trapezes were hung from the track in the barn's peak and we learned to pump with our knees, hang by our ankles and swan dive into the soft, springy hay.

My favourite set-up was a series of dangling ropes with knots at the ends that you pretended were jungle vines as you swung from mow to mow, re-enacting the tales of Edgar Rice Burroughs.

The hay mow was a secluded place to go on a soggy Saturday to read adventure books, dream of far away places, then slip into a lazy sleep to the accompaniment of tattooing raindrops on the tin roof.

Later on, in our teen-age years, these quiet and comfortable hide-aways became the "perfumed garden" where you held hands and shared that first kiss with the neighbour's daughter or visiting city girl.

I understand and appreciate the changes in modern hay-gathering and storing, but when I see those

huge coils in the barnyard exposed to
the elements or covered with black
vinyl, I wonder what has become of
the hay mows of Canada? Are they
filled with mouldy bales or rusting
machinery? Have they been turned
into rural badminton courts or
bowling alleys?

Perhaps they are simply abandoned
places, haunted by the ghostly
sounds of joyful laughter, Tarzan yells
and tender murmuring of youthful
acquiescence.

There are people who will tell you that there is just
as much romance to be found by a young person in
the city as in a rural environment and they may be
right. Roller skating, bicycling, street hockey and
skateboarding do not lend themselves to gravel
roads or country lanes. Ice cream parlours, Saturday
matinees and pool halls were not part of my youth.
The charm of the video arcade or shopping mall for
today's youngsters is entirely a city phenomenon.

But, given a choice, wouldn't you rather roll
down a daisy-covered hill until your whole being is
suffused with a dizzying sense of sky, earth, grass and
leaves? Wouldn't you sooner lie on your belly at the
edge of a summer creek and study a tadpole as its
gills close and its limbs form? Or, wouldn't you like
to actually get lost in a woods and experience that
tingling thrill of panic when you wonder whether or
not moss really only grows on the north side of a
tree? I would.

NEIGHBOURS

Anyone with access to a woodlot should investigate its wonders these first weeks of June. Springing up from the moist, damp, dark earth are carpets of wildflowers to excite the eye and stir the heart.

Trilliums lead the way in waves of white and pockets of deep red. Then come the adder tongues, those curling, spotted beauties that nestle close to the trees and old stumps. Mayflowers still linger and cowslips are giving their final burst of yellow to the sides of creeks. Wild violets are in full bloom, shyly peeking out from under mossy logs and old leaves. But by far the loveliest to my eye are the phlox.

Ranging in colours from delicate pale blue to deep vibrant purple, phlox gather in clumps where the sun manages to filter through the treetops. Unlike many other wildflowers, phlox can be picked with little damage to the root system, making them attractive bouquets for the springtime kitchen table. They were also responsible for my one and only dog bite.

My route to public school took me through a twenty-acre wood at the back of our farm, over several of the neighbours' pasture and grain fields up Hogle's Hill to the second concession and down it to the old schoolhouse, a distance of about three miles. I came to know every tree, rock, fence and creek intimately in the many years I walked to and fro.

I had nine brothers and sisters who had hiked the trail to school before me, but the next oldest to me finished the year I started. This meant I walked alone. It also meant that an old family tradition fell solely to my care.

Nobody remembered how it started, but every year when phlox appeared in our woods, a generous bunch would be taken to Mrs. Hogle at the farm on the top of the hill. She loved their frail beauty and gentle fragrance. I like to think we did it for the sheer joy of sharing and not for the inevitable treats the kindly old lady gave us in return. Regardless, when I was seven and reported the arrival of the spring flowers in our woods, I needed no urging by my older siblings to do my duty.

I left early that morning to allow time to pick a large garland and, after knocking at the door, stood expectantly on the Hogle stoop. Suddenly, from around the corner of the house, their dog silently and swiftly leaped up behind me and sunk his teeth into my leg. I screamed with fright and pain and ran howling down the lane scattering school books and blue blossoms. Mr. Hogle came running from the barn across the road, wrapped me in his arms and tried to comfort me.

Later that day, as the pain in my bandaged and poulticed leg was subsiding, my mother sat beside me on the bed and explained, "Some other kids have been hitting the dog with stones and teasing him with sticks. It's not really the dog's fault, you know. It probably mistook you for one of them. Mr. Hogle says he'll shoot the dog if we feel he should. I said I would ask what you think."

"I don't know."

"Of course, no one wants a dangerous dog around, even though it is a very good cow-dog and has never bitten anyone before. What should we tell Mr. Hogle?"

"I don't know."

"Whatever you decide, it's important that you not let this make you afraid of dogs. It's like getting back on a horse after you've fallen off. I think you should see the dog again.

There's also one other important fact."

"What's that?"

"Mrs. Hogle never did get her phlox."

After a few days I was able to walk to school again. The dog spotted me before I reached the Hogle land, but his bounding leaps and wagging tail told me there was nothing to fear. He licked my face and sniffed my lunch pail. I opened it and gave him half a honey sandwich. Then I exchanged an armful of phlox for a wedge of chocolate cake with a fearful but smiling Mrs. Hogle.

Over the years I delivered a lot of those beautiful flowers and accepted many cookies, mugs of lemonade and, once, a huge bag of peanuts in their shells that had come all the way from Georgia. The dog became a good friend and used to see me part way home through the woods during the dark fall and winter nights. I still have a scar on my leg after all these years, but I've never had a fear of dogs. And, I share with Mrs. Hogle a deep love of wild phlox.

Slowly but surely over the years, the woods and fields of our rural community have given way to the encroachment of a modern society and its demand for better transportation and communication.

When the section of Highway 401, from Toronto to Kingston, was constructed in the fifties, it sliced acres off my neighbours' farms. Some were cut in half and, since access could only be gained to the severed parts by a designated overpass, these unfortunate farmers were forced to travel many miles in order to tend land that was in reality only a few yards away. County roads were turned into highways. Municipal governments expropriated additional footage from the farmers' fields. Hydro towers blossomed and swaths of trees were felled to accommodate the plethora of overhead wires. Microwave relay stations and radar installations became part of the rural landscape. There is hardly a farm in the Quinte area left unscarred. Such is the price of progress and it will likely continue until our lush and fertile fields disappear under layers of asphalt and our tree branches give way to steel cables as the resting place for birds.

I imagine our pioneer farmers saw this coming when the railway went through.

THE RAILWAY

With the cutbacks and even cancellation of Via Rail lines, we are hearing a lot these days about the romance of train travel. For some people, it is the only way to go and it conjures up memories of steam engines, luxury dining cars and the clickety-clack of iron wheels. I don't get that excited about riding on a train, even though, or maybe because, most of my younger days were spent living next to the tracks.

We had two railway lines running through our farm. CPR had a single track on the south end that was used for shunting trains between Trenton and Belleville, but the CNR ran just one hundred yards in front of our house and was a large part of our family's daily life.

It was important to memorize the train schedule because we crossed the tracks several times each day with hay wagons, manure spreaders and herds of cows on their way to pasture. The rail line was divided into two- or three-mile strips maintained by a crew of "section men," who kept their equipment and personal belongings in a "section house," a red wooden shack just in front of our place. A job with the railroad was a much sought after position in the thirties when regular employment was scarce.

They were a hardy breed of men who cleared the snow and kept the frost-loosened spikes secure in the bitter winter weather and in the sweltering heat of summer swung

DESERONTO PUBLIC LIBRARY

their hammers in co-ordinated rhythm to lay new rails and ties. Their daily presence made them a part of our family. From the time I was old enough to walk, I ran errands for them — taking them messages, filling their water jugs from the farm spring and keeping an eye on the smouldering grass they burned along the rail beds. In return, they would share the contents of their enormous lunch buckets with me and give me little treasures like toys and books that had fallen out of open passenger train windows.

The biggest thrill of all was when I started school and the workers would let me ride part of the way on the jiggers and hand-cars. Jiggers were motorized and *put-putted* their way down the track at what I thought was great speed. The handcars had to be pumped, usually by four men, and when they let me have a turn, the handles would lift me off my feet.

Overnight visitors to our home woke up terrified when a fast train thundered by, whistle screaming. The rest of us were so attuned to the schedule and the noise we never stirred even though the house shook and the piercing light swept across our bedroom walls.

Summers during the depression brought the "rail rodders" or "gentlemen of the road." They were mostly heading west looking for work and could be seen sitting in every empty boxcar that went by. Some preferred to perch on top of the cars to pick up what breeze they could, despite the flying cinders from the smoke-stack. One of them had painted an "X" on a fence post near our farm, which meant this was a place they could get a hand-out. My father complained quite a bit but I think secretly didn't mind because he knew my mother would turn no one away. She could give them plates of home-made bread, cheese, a piece of pie or some apples. Sometimes they would offer to split some wood or do a bit of hoeing in payment for the meal. Far more important for me was the chance to hear their stories.

There were the professional tramps who had travelled the length and breadth of North America. They told me tales of cotton picking in Georgia, grubbing for gold in California, fishing off the Grand Banks and being chased by railway detectives in cities from San Francisco to Halifax. I heard about the great rail lines – the Baltimore and Ohio, the Delaware and Lackawana, the Union Pacific and the famous Atchison, Topeka and the Sante Fe. Most, however, were down-on-their-luck Canadians looking for a job, needing a bath, a meal or someplace to sleep. Many homes along the railway kept a "hobo couch" on their back verandah for these interesting visitors. Ours now has an honoured spot in my living room.

In June of 1939 King George VI and Queen Elizabeth toured Canada by train. The royal coach zipped past our house about seven o'clock at night. No one believed me when I said I saw them sitting at one of the windows. I did have something to show, though. I had sneaked down to the track earlier and stuck a few pennies on the rails and for years after carried the coins as souvenirs flattened by the king and queen of England.

They were not all pleasant memories. We lost several animals that had broken through the fence and wandered onto the tracks. Some section men were hurt when they were unable to move equipment off the rails in time. One spectacular train wreck saw a freight of ninety grain cars derailed within sight of our home. No one was severely injured, but for many springs after, wheat was still sprouting in our swamp. Local farmers were told to salvage what they could from the wreck. My father and brothers gathered up several twisted steel doors from the boxcars, straightened them out and made a new roof for our machine shed.

I drove past the old farm not long ago. The timbers and boards on the shed are fairly decayed, but fifty years later, the roof still looks fine.

July

July

Two of my children, Mandy and Lesley, have chosen to live and raise their families on a farm. My son, Steven, while not actually on a farm, does live in the country. Rural life in our family seems to be contagious. My sister Flossie lives on a farm just three concessions north of me. My brother Bert, after many years in the city, has bought a farm on which to spend his retirement years. He has converted the barn into a comfortable woodworking shop and his pride and joy is a huge farm pond that is a favourite spot for hundreds of Canada geese and wild ducks.

A while ago Mandy was visiting Bert and he asked her, "Why did your father ever decide to move back to a farm? When he was a boy, he hated farm life." Mandy answered, "I think he loved living on a farm. It was the work he hated." She was absolutely right.

There is nothing enjoyable about getting up at six in the morning, milking cows by hand, pitching hay and lugging grain, carrying water, shovelling manure and doing the back-breaking and mind-numbing labour that was a daily grind in the thirties and forties.

Very few farms in our area had tractors and the sophisticated machinery we see today simply hadn't been invented yet. Horses pulled the ploughs, mowers, rakes and binders, and it was human strength that did the lifting, digging, carrying and pulling. When we look at today's modern farm tractor with its enclosed cab that is heated in the winter and air-conditioned in the summer, equipped with push-button hydraulics and power take-off, able to plough or harvest an average size farm in a single day, we begin to appreciate the role of the horse in yesterday's agriculture.

My father was proud of our horses. He bred and trained them to a fine-tuned performance, gentle yet spirited, eager to work singly or in two-, four- or five-horse teams. Gilbert, the iron-grey Percheron stud, was of show-horse calibre, winning ribbons annually at local exhibitions and the big Royal Winter Fair in Toronto.

The whole family would spend hours washing and currycombing his coat to a brilliant sheen, plaiting tiny paper roses in his mane and forelock and polishing his hooves until they glowed. He sired many foals throughout the countryside but, for me, his finest achievement was "the old grey mare," as she was known by friends and neighbours. Our family called her Floss and she was born the same year as me. She grew to be a strong and quiet brood mare with numerous offspring. She was also blind.

Her inability to see made her dependent on the other horses, especially when in double harness. Mostly she was teamed with her son King, a huge bay gelding who had more brawn than brains. King liked to cause trouble and had, I swear, a weird sense of humour. One of his favourite tricks was to drink deeply from the spring after being led to water and retain the last mouthful until being tied once again in his stall. Then he would open his lips and send a stream of water gushing down your neck. Since most of us knew enough to step quickly out of the way, his water prank only worked on unsuspecting visitors who had been conned into taking him out for a drink. King and Floss together accounted for most of our spectacular "runaways."

A runaway team dragging a piece of machinery behind was a terrifying experience dreaded by every farmer. We certainly had our share. Part of the reason was Dad's training methods. He believed in breaking a horse to the point of obedience but never damaging the animal's spirit. Consequently, most of our horses were "on the edge," always ready for adventure and King seemed especially primed to oblige.

One day, on the far south side of the farm, the wheel of the hay-mower hit a woodchuck hole, causing the tongue to swing wildly and hit King on his rear leg. This was all the excuse he needed. Off like a shot with Floss following his lead, he plunged across the field through the fence and down the gravel road toward home, the cutting bar slicing everything in its path for nearly two miles. They stopped, panting, by the stable door, the mower a twisted mass of steel, the harness in shreds and my brothers and I trudging forlornly through the clouds of dust, cursing the day King was born.

One winter afternoon, Bert and I were drawing manure, the regular cold weather occupation that entailed pitching the steaming, stinking mountains of shit that stood near the stables onto the sleigh for transportation to the snow-covered fields. There it was spread by forkfuls as far as we could throw, turning acres of pristine white into brown carpets of fertilizer.

The sleigh was about twenty feet long and six feet wide. When loaded, it held nearly half a ton. We had just completed stacking the final load of the day when something frightened King. With a lurch the sleigh started forward. Bert grabbed at the lines, slipped on a cow flop and missed our last chance to stop the team. They broke into a gallop and headed down the lane straight toward the railway tracks. By the time they reached the crossing, King was running flat out with chunks of manure flying, sleigh bells chiming and Floss gamely keeping pace. They hit the gate head on, flattened it and kept on going. The force of crashing the gate split the sleigh in two and the whole load of manure collapsed and settled across both rails of the CNR main line. By the time we caught up to them, the horses stood tangled in harness, snorting steamy billows of breath into the frosty air. We unhitched them from the wreckage and returned them to the stable. Then Bert remembered, "My God, the six o'clock Flyer is due in twenty minutes."

We grabbed our forks and raced back to the tracks. A frenzy of pitching with a strength we didn't know we possessed resulted in finally uncovering the gleaming rails just seconds before the non-stop express from Toronto to Montreal roared through.

But for me the most memorable runaway was

at hay-raking time. This is a job the youngest member of the family usually inherits as soon as he learns to drive horses. You sit on a high seat over long curved tines that rake the hay into bundles. A tripping mechanism is activated with the foot to dump the coiled hay into long windrows stretching the length of the field. It's not that hard a job and with the rake being light and mounted on two high wheels, it is easy for the horses to pull.

We had just finished the noon meal when my Dad told the hired man to bring the rake around to the lane and for me to take over the job for the afternoon. I climbed up on one side of the rake as he prepared to step off the other. Whether it was our combined weight or faulty workmanship, the tongue suddenly snapped. The sound of the wooden tongue splitting startled King and he was off again. The team lunged forward spilling the hired man into the lane and toppling me forward between the horses where I managed to hold onto only one line. I missed the horses' hooves, but as I fell through the rake to the gravel road, my pant leg tripped the gear that released the tines. The last thing I remember was yanking the one line which caused blind Floss to turn in a harmless circle. Then everything faded to black as one of the tines went into my back and another pierced my head.

When I came to, my mother was stripping off my blood-soaked shirt and wiping gravel from my wounds. Bert was hurriedly getting the car ready to drive me to the doctor in Trenton; the horses had circled their way into an apple tree and stood placidly gazing back at another runaway victim.

It was one of those "It could have been a lot worse" accidents. My head and back healed readily enough but even today, after all those years, whenever a new barber tackles my hair, I hear, "That's a nasty scar you have there. An old war wound?"

"You might say that," I answer. "It was my final cavalry charge."

I don't recall ever driving horses after that. It wasn't that the incident made me frightened of them, because in later years I owned several horses though they were strictly for pleasure riding. I considered the farm draught-horse, taught to obey and slave without question, a symbol of grinding toil that I didn't want for myself or my family. While mechanized farming has taken away a great deal of the drudgery, it is still for many a morning-'til-night, seven-days-a-week existence with very little compensation.

THE VISITORS

Adults say vacation, kids call them holidays and July is the month for both. The echo of school doors closing almost blends with the starting motors of cars, vans, planes and boats as a nation heads for anywhere, as long as it's away from home.

Until I began drawing a weekly pay cheque, I didn't have to worry about what to do in the summer. Being born into a farm family precluded any thought of summer holidays.

Cows still had to be milked twice a day, seven days a week. Peas, beans and berries ripened in the July sun and weeds knew nothing about time off.

With the exception of the Junior Farmers' weiner roast at Oak Lake near Stirling or the Sunday School picnic at the Sandbanks near Picton, it was like any other month, only hotter.

Actually there was one other day that was special in my pre-teen years. On the first Sunday in July we would pack a hamper with food and lemonade, squeeze into the family car and drive all the way to Cobourg. This was before the 401, so thirty miles per hour on the Number Two Highway in a temperamental old Nash was quite the trip.

I had a much older brother who lived in Rochester, New York, and each year he and my sister-in-law brought their two children, Fred and Shirley, over to Cobourg by excursion boat so they could spend their summer holidays on their grand-parents' farm. The excitement of waiting for the boat to come was the highlight of my day. The sandy beach was fun, Mom's potato salad, cold roast beef and home-made bread undeniably delicious. Even wading in the icy water of Lake Ontario was a thrill, but my eyes seldom left the horizon. There, where the pale blue sky blended with the darker shade of the largest expanse of water I had ever seen, would come the huge *Ontario* I or *Ontario* II from Rochester. Well, I guess they weren't huge, but then neither was I.

First you would spot a wisp of smoke, then the black smoke-stack would come into view and finally the gleaming white of the upper deck sparkled in the sun and grew larger. My father always said the same thing: "That's how we know the world is round." I was not so much amazed by this physical fact as I was by the inference that my father was so much smarter than all those people before Columbus who thought the world was flat.

We would hurry and join the crowd at the pier and, as the boat docked, anxiously scan the faces of the passengers leaning over the rail to spot our Yankee visitors.

Americans seemed strangely foreign to me in those days. They talked funny. They had a nasal twang and pronounced New York "*Noo Yawk.*" The adults sported brightly coloured shirts, smoked cigarettes called Chesterfield and Lucky Strike and grumbled about a man named Roosevelt. The kids didn't brush their teeth with baking soda but had tubes of paste called Kolynos and Ipana. They ate Baby Ruth chocolate bars and they wore underwear. To a farm kid underwear meant long johns worn in the cold weather. To have anything between you and your overalls in July seemed ludicrous.

Fred was only two years younger than I and Shirley a year younger than that, so we were more like chums than relatives. There was no thought of calling me Uncle Roy. Most of the time we got along fine, but, as the summer dragged on, I would begin to resent the fact that they were on holidays while I worked. When they tired of the "fun" of stook-pitching or picking worms off the tomato plants, they could lie in the shade or listen to the radio while I still had my chores to do. When I became particularly rankled, I would suggest to Fred he might like to learn how to milk a cow. Then I would seat him beside old Belle, knowing that at the first touch of strange fingers on her teats, she would send pail, stool and boy flying with a no-nonsense kick. It wasn't a very hospitable way to treat a guest, I suppose, but it gave him a good story to tell his city friends when he returned.

I was on my best behaviour as the holiday season drew to a close so I would not be denied the trip back to Cobourg. There, standing on the pier, I would wave goodbye and watch the boat become smaller until finally the smoke disappeared into the lake.

A couple of years ago, I stopped in at the waterfront in Cobourg. They've kept it in good shape. Gabions have been placed along the shoreline to prevent erosion. The sand, grass and picnic facilities have been carefully tended. Everything looks much the same, only smaller.

Maybe this July I'll take my grand-children there. It's only half an hour on the freeway. *Ontario* I and *Ontario* II are long gone, but perhaps we will spot a laker plying its trade from the U.S. to the Canadian shore. To kids who have seen photographs of our planet taken from outer space, it won't make much of an impression, but I'll tell them how we really know the world is round.

Then again, I'm not even sure boats have smoke-stacks anymore.

The family farm extended from the shores of the Bay of Quinte to almost the second concession of Sidney Township. It was given to the Bonisteel family by a grateful Crown, as were most United Empire Loyalist farms, in appreciation of support during the American Revolution. It was about four hundred acres in size with one large, comfortable home overlooking the bay and a second, draughty, ramshackled structure built by my blind grandfather on the back half. It was on this back or north farm that I grew up and I learned alternately to love and hate it. It was, for the most part, good fertile land with lush pastures for our dairy cows and work-horses, orchards of apples, plums, pears and cherries. It also contained acres of clay loam for our grain and hay crops, plus a good sized woodlot of maple, ash, oak and towering pine. Two railway tracks crossed the property from east to west and a large creek, a habitat for pike, suckers and mudcats, meandered diagonally through the swampland all the way to the bay.

Our house was at the very end of a dead-end gravel road, about a mile from the nearest side-road and half-way between the Front, which is what the Bayside area was called, and the second concession of Sidney Township. While we were surrounded by farming neighbours, no other house or building was visible from ours. The remoteness was made more acute by not having a telephone or electricity. When hydro finally came in the late forties, it was first installed only in the barn, where my father reasoned the need was greatest.

The original farm was handed down to my father and his twin brother Willy. The only thing these two men ever had in common was being born on the same day. Benson, my father, was tall and rangy with a luxuriant head of hair, generous and exceedingly worldly. Uncle Willy was fine-featured, completely bald, God-fearing and so parsimonious he squeaked. He lived off his parents' money before they died and his inheritance after. Never one to rush into things, he waited until he was fifty-two to marry. My father meanwhile had left the security of the homestead to carve out a future for his ever-expanding family in a variety of unprofitable pursuits. By 1930 the depression left him no option but to return hat in hand like a prodigal son seeking his birthright. Unlike his biblical predecessor, no fatted calf was killed nor ring put on his finger. He would have to buy the back half of the farm from his twin brother and make the old second house livable for his family, including the new baby, Roy. Many years later, when I would ask why Uncle Willy was sending men to haul out wagon loads of prime timber from our woods, I was told it was in lieu of that year's mortgage money, which could not be met. Up until he retired from farming in 1957, my father made yearly payments to his brother.

Marriage, widowerhood, remarriage and the birth of three fine sons mellowed my uncle somewhat and he became a kinder, more accepting person. Some habits, though, never change. In the early fifties when I was an announcer on the Belleville radio station, I ran a contest during the Christmas season that awarded a free turkey each day to listeners whose names were drawn at random from letters received at the station. I was surprised one day to find a note from my uncle asking if I could visit him. When I arrived at his house, he made me a cup of tea, inquired about my parents and then told me why he had written.

"It's about those free turkeys. I was wondering if you could get me one."

"I couldn't do that, Uncle Willy. Family members of the radio staff are not eligible. How would it sound if I read over the air that a Bonisteel had won?"

"I don't see what difference it makes. It isn't as though we were in the same family."

Even though I tried very hard to explain the situation, I knew when I left that he was disappointed. A few days later, when our turkey supplier arrived, I bought an extra one from him for eight dollars of my own money and had it delivered to Uncle Willy's house, along with a card wishing him a Merry Christmas from his loving nephew. I don't know whether he knew I paid for it or if he thought he had won it. I never saw or heard from him again.

SIMPLE THINGS

According to the *Farmer's Almanac*, our summers are getting hotter and more uncomfortable. Old-timers who have lived through many hot spells in the Quinte area agree. They tell me there has been no precedent for the stifling, humid mosquito-infested days we are now experiencing.

"Those lazy, hazy, crazy days of summer" that Nat King Cole used to sing about have driven us inside our houses to seek relief with central air conditioning, electric fans and ice cubes. While enjoying the benefits of modern technology, I often think back to a time when we were dependent on our own imagination and initiative to beat the heat.

Growing up on a farm with no electricity meant never having a refrigerator or a freezer. We didn't even have an icebox. What we did have was an ice-house. These were built to store blocks of ice, cut with long saws from the bay during the winter and packed in layers of sawdust to retard thawing. During the hot weather, chunks were chipped off the main blocks, placed in a long, narrow "shot-gun" can and immersed in forty-gallon drums of warm milk. This kept the milk fresh and sweet for delivery to the cheese factory the next morning.

The ice-house provided a wonderful way to keep cool for playful kids as we climbed all over the mountain of clammy sawdust in a summer game of tag. Pieces of ice were also used, along with a few cups of rock salt, to fill up the sides of the family ice-cream maker on Saturday night, when an hour of frantic cranking produced another delicious way of cooling off.

Food preservation in warm weather took extra effort. Hams were smoked, side pork salted, beef dried, chicken either eaten fresh or sometimes cooked and canned in mason jars. Butter was churned, stored in crocks in the cellar, with the buttermilk making a refreshing summer drink. The "Raleigh man" made regular visits to the farm with bottles of orange and lemon extract, which, when mixed with well water, almost tasted like the genuine article.

We had two dug wells near the house and barn where any number of items could be lowered to keep cool, including a small boy who not only liked the dark chill of the stone walls but enjoyed looking back up through the opening to see the stars in the noonday sky.

The best and coldest water was found in a small spring hidden by willow trees and reeds near the creek in our south field. Years before, someone had sunk a stout barrel around the bubbling oasis in order to trap water so cold it made your teeth ache when you drank.

One hot July day, when I was about twelve, I was hoeing pumpkins near the south field when I heard a voice calling. I looked up and saw what seemed to be an apparition coming through the blur of heat waves that clung close to the ground. A man, well into his seventies, dressed in a straw boater, white shirt, white suit, and white shoes was approaching. He carried a silver-handled cane and as he drew near took a large white handkerchief from his pocket and mopped the only bit of colour he had — a red, sweating face. Since we were far from any road, he must have walked several miles.

"I gather you live here."

"Yessir."

"I was the hired man once for the fellow who owned this farm. We called him blind Billy. 'Spect he's dead now."

"That was my grandfather. He died before I was born."

"Good man. Gave me a job when I needed one. I went west. Got into the lumber business. Live in Victoria now. Know where that is?"

"British Columbia."

"Smart lad. Bet you know where the spring is. Used to be a spring near here. Best water I ever tasted."

I laid down my hoe and led him to the bottom of the field through the trees and grass to the hidden spring. Ignoring his white suit, he sat on the damp, marshy sod. I handed him the old tin dipper that always hung on a stake nearby and watched him lift it brimming full to his lips. His eyes closed in ecstasy as he savoured every drop.

"Been fifty years since I sat here. Been all over the world. Lots of money in lumber. Thought I'd take a last trip. Visit places I remember. 'Spect it sounds foolish to you, lad. When you get old, you'll understand. When you get old, you remember simple things like this." He reached the dipper once more into the spring. "Best damned water I ever tasted."

I understand what he meant.

We were not what you would call a close-knit family. Because of the disparity in our ages, I seldom saw my older brothers and sisters. One brother had left many years before to live in Rochester, New York. Two brothers farmed at Wainfleet on the shores of Lake Erie. One brother was a travelling salesman whose address was anywhere he hung his hat in North America. Two sisters had married and moved away while I was still a baby. My brother Jack was in high school before I was in primary and he later joined the

RCAF. That left Bert and Flossie as the ones who shared my early years. Some of the others came home at Christmas or during their summer vacation periods. Some we only saw at funerals or weddings. All kept in touch by mail.

My parents died within a year of each other. While sorting through their effects, I found boxes of letters and cards that had been lovingly saved. Over sixty years of history was recorded in newsy missives telling of places visited, illnesses survived, children born, current weather conditions and requests for a few dollars to "tide us over."

The last thing I need are more cartons to store in an already over-crowded attic, but for some reason I just can't throw them out.

THE MAILBOX

The days of the individual mailbox appear to be numbered. Families in the suburbs are now being instructed to pick up their regular deliveries from communal green compartments at a central location. Can the old country mailbox sitting proudly on its weathered post be far behind?

Nothing says "country" like the rural mailbox. It comes in two sizes, small and large, with a flap in front that lets in snow in the winter and nest-building starlings in the summer. You can always tell the families that have moved from the city to play farmer. Their receptacles are mounted on welded links of chain or metal cream cans planted with geraniums and their names are stencilled on cute little wooden plaques.

It takes years for a mailbox to develop character. The post becomes grey and mossy, the box rusts and chips around the edges, the flap gives a welcoming squeal when opened and the red flag turns brown and droops. Unfortunately they seldom last long enough to mature. Mailbox bashing by city kids with a car and a baseball bat has become a popular sport.

Our family never had a telephone when I was a boy and the only way to keep in touch with relatives, friends or indeed the outside world was through the little metal box at the end of the lane. Everyone seemed to write letters in those days, even children. I had letters to write to cousins describing a new tree-house or complaining about schoolwork. Then there were the thank-you letters to uncles and aunts for birthday or Christmas gifts. Pen-pals were a popular fad and I had one in far off Manitoba.

Most of my correspondence involved sending bundles of cereal box tops to Battle Creek, Michigan, in exchange for jack-knives, secret code rings and official junior officer badges in the Dick Tracy Detective Club. I breakfasted my way from Private to Inspector and topped off my law enforcement career by winning a genuine, simulated, two-way radio.

Most of the mail, of course, was for my parents. Besides letter and post-cards they regularly received the day-late local paper, the *Farmer's Advocate*, the *Canadian Countryman*, and the *Family Herald*. My father for some reason also subscribed to the *Winnipeg Free Press*. It must have been heavy in farm news though I seldom got past the comics. When Mary O'Hara's *My Friend Flicka* was serialized in one of these papers, I remember haunting the mailbox for days and reading each thrilling installment right there on the grass, leaning against the post.

Our mailman was Mr. Stickle. He never owned a car. In the summer, he delivered by horse and buggy and in the winter by horse and cutter. He sorted mail as he went, his horse familiar enough with the route to pull up and stop at the right distance from each box without direction.

There was no junk mail or unsolicited books to send back. There was also no need to go to the post office to buy stamps. You simply piled six pennies on top of each letter in the box and Mr. Stickle did the rest.

The joys of sending and receiving hand-written letters have faded in a world of electronic communication. In the name of efficiency and apparent economy, the mail will no longer come to us. We will go to it and find material we never wanted and won't read. The country mailbox that delighted the farmer and directed the visitor will go the way of Mr. Stickle's horse. It would likely be too difficult to stack forty pennies neatly inside a rusting metal box anyway.

August

August

I suppose there are people today, certainly members of the younger generation, who would have no idea what Mr. Stickle's cutter looked like. It was a one-horse sleigh with narrow runners and a cushioned seat that was a means of speedy transportation during the winter. Its summer counterpart was the buggy, which had four large wheels and a canopy, or the democrat, which was just an elongated buggy with a box-like body for carrying light loads. I still own a cutter and buggy and when I look at them, I realize the many pieces of farm equipment that have become obsolete.

Only in agricultural museums are you likely to find a binder or a thresher – two machines that became one, the combine. A corn binder tied the stalks together into sheaves for easier transportation to the barn. This gave way to the forage harvester, which chopped the corn while still in the field.

In the plough department were the gang ploughs, which had what were called mouldboards – curved metal plates that turned the earth. If you used a gang plough, you could expect your legs to ache at the end of the day because there was no place on the machine to sit. The sulky plough, on the other hand, had a seat similar to sulkies used in standardbred racing today.

After the plough came the cultivator. Older models were straight-toothed and dug into the ploughed furrows to level the earth. The spring-toothed cultivator was an improvement in that its teeth did not break as easily and could be individually replaced if they did. Following the cultivator were the drags, or harrows, with their wide, spiked frame that cleared off debris and smoothed the ground in preparation for the seed drill.

One of the most back-breaking jobs I knew was sawing trees and logs with the cross-cut saw. This jagged-toothed torture device was about seven feet long with handles at both ends, requiring two people to pull back and forth until either the tree gave out or they did. Chain-saws must have been invented by a desperate cross-cutting woodsman.

Now and again at county fairs you can find a display of old farm equipment. I've even seen cross-cut saws decorating the walls of fancy restaurants in the city. For some of us, they nudge old memories of an earlier day, which quickly give way to feelings of relief that they are no longer part of our daily lives.

They also remind us of jobs we had that have also disappeared.

COW WATCHING

There is no category in the employ-ment market these days for cow watching. Not that it ever was a major career choice for Canada's farm youth, but it was an indispensable job during August on the mixed farms of the early forties.

As the dog days set in, the traditional pastureland became overcropped and brown. Hay-fields that had already given up one offering of alfalfa and clover were now starting a second crop, which made excellent day-time grazing for the dairy cattle.

Unfortunately, these areas were always adjacent to other fields that grew wheat and oats now just heading out in plump kernels; or corn about as high as a heifer's eye — green, succulent and forming small juicy ears.

The problem was fencing. Especially during the war years when wire, staples, steel posts and farm workers were very hard to come by. Without proper fencing, nothing stood between the hungry Holsteins and the maturing fields of grain — nothing except the cow watcher.

What a job! The perfect pursuit for a young lad who was not overly ambitious and preferred reading books under a shade tree to hoeing tomatoes, yet enjoyed the feeling that comes with performing a vital and necessary role.

One had to be fleet of foot. Cows are canny beasts. Especially old Belle. She was a big-boned purebred with an udder the size of a picnic basket. She was the undisputed leader of our herd of twenty-five, which followed her every move.

With a nonchalant air she would steadily chew her way closer and closer to the fenceless boundary. One long-lashed eye would occasionally flick in my direction to see if I was paying attention. If our eyes met, she would casually continue munching as though she had nothing on her mind but the clump of grass under her nose.

You could see her measuring the distance to the forbidden fodder and when she sensed an advantage, she would lengthen her stride and charge. With the herd plunging after her, she could flatten more grain or corn in two minutes than a combine could in half a day.

My downfall was books. Sheltered from the August sun by towering hickories and oaks I fought the Spanish civil war with Ernest Hemingway; explored the intimate secrets of China with Pearl S. Buck; and was a voyeur of the Deep South with Erskine Caldwell. Belle seemed to know when I became more interested in Pilar, Wang Lung or Jeeter than in her. She seemed aware that only the sound of crunching cornstalks would bring me back to reality.

I obviously had to find less riveting material. My sister subscribed to an American magazine called *Movie Stories*. It printed condensations of the latest movie scripts, and although I enjoyed reading the plots of *How Green Was My Valley*, *Mrs. Miniver*, *The Maltese Falcon* and other current releases, the writing was not as engrossing, which meant I could keep a sharper eye on my grazing charges.

Then somebody invented the electric fence. This put an end to watching cows. There was no need for normal electrical service, which for us was many years away. From a dry cell battery, a single wire could be quickly strung around the protected fields and one touch with a damp nose persuaded the bravest of animals to back off.

My father, always ready to take advantage of the newest technology, especially if it meant freeing up young manpower, was quick to invest in this ever-alert electric guardian. Wooden stakes were hammered into the ground, the insulators attached and in a couple of days August became just another month.

Oh, it was fun for a while tricking city visitors into touching the wire with a dewy blade of grass, and my mother claimed that grabbing the hot wire now and then was good for her arthritis, but Belle was very upset. She wouldn't even let me milk her for a whole week. I, of course, resented my return to the tomato patch.

But now and again on winter nights when I'm passing time with old forties movies on TV, my mind recalls those published scripts. While Rick tells Sam, "You played it for her – now play it for me," I'm in a different scenario. It's a long hot August scene scored by bumble-bees and cicadas. The plot is simple. A young boy is matching wits and exchanging furtive glances with a determined and envious old Holstein cow.

My mother had a long life. She died at eighty-eight. I would like to be able to say it was a good life, but certainly her married years were hard and often disappointing. Ten children, back-breaking work on a farm with no modern conveniences and always living below what we would now consider the poverty line, does not the grand existence make. As the youngest, I remember her as old and world-weary before her

time. For her, one day was very much like the last –
the months, seasons and years a continuum of work,
obligations and survival. Yet I have never known
anyone with such an indomitable spirit, open
generosity and joyous humour. She showed her
children what it was to have pride with humility,
intelligence with purpose and unconditional love.

She maintained a schizophrenic approach to
life. While her hands were kneading bread or her feet
climbing ladders, her heart was full of song. Three
years of high school completed her formal education,
but her mind had been opened to the wonders of
literature. Long before I understood the meaning of
her words, she was reciting Longfellow, Tennyson,
and Shakespeare to me as other mothers would have
read Beatrix Potter. She answered boyhood questions
with literary quotes, tossing in authors' names with a
familiarity I have only heard since from English
professors.

"Mom, why do I have to do all this homework?"

"Because, as Gibbon says, 'The winds and
waves are always on the side of the ablest navi-
gators.'"

It was never enough for her to just shake you
out of your sleep in the morning with "Get up. It's
time for school." It was always something like:

Wake now my Love! Awake. For it is time.
The rosy morn long since left Tithon's bed,
All ready to her silver coach to climb,
And Phoebus 'gins to show her glorious
    head.

It was many years later shuffling through musty books in some television research project that I realized she had been reciting Edmund Spenser.

One of her favourites was Thomas Gray's "Elegy Written in a Country Churchyard." She knew all thirty-two verses by heart and would lustily recite it at the slightest provocation. If we were hoeing together in the fields and I complained about the hard work or the lack of money, she would pause, lean on her hoe and intone:

> Let not Ambition mock their useful toil,
> Their homely joys, and destiny obscure;
> Nor Grandeur hear with a disdainful
>   smile
> The short and simple annals of the poor.

And if I questioned the fairness of not being recognized for something I had done or wanted praise for schoolwork I thought outstanding, she would placate me with:

> Full many a gem of purest ray serene,
> The dark unfathom'd caves of ocean bear:
> Full many a flower is born to blush
>   unseen,
> And waste its sweetness on the desert air.

Quotes from Thomas Gray were not very satisfying responses to a young boy's confusion and yet, even then, I think I realized it was her way of keeping sane and holding on to a little bit of beauty in a harsh environment.

Her poetry stayed with her but her children didn't. Almost all of us left home while still in our teens. There was just no future on the farm. My father had many good qualities, but working in harmony with his children was not one of them. By contrast, my mother had the knack of getting along with everyone. She also had a sense of precognition. Most of the time when we came back home it was without advance warning. My parents' lack of a telephone was partly responsible. Late at night, at the sound of the first footstep in the darkened farm kitchen, my mother's voice would be heard from her upstairs bedroom correctly identifying the visitor. A long-time friend of mine, Bill Scott, recalls with amazement the times when, needing a haven for the night, he would tiptoe through the unlocked door of the farmhouse to be greeted by my mother's voice from above calling, "Is that you, Billy?" She never missed.

She was the great-great-granddaughter of Captain John Meyers, the Canadian patriot, British spy, disputed hero of the war of 1812 and founder of the city of Belleville. While this gave her no particular pride, it did give her the opportunity to tell with some authority the many tales associated with this fascinating pioneer. His narrow escape from the American forces in the 1770s, his long trek on foot from Duchess County, New York, to Canada, his escapades with General Burgoyne at the surrender of Saratoga, his attempt to kidnap the American General Schuyler at Albany, his release of the black Loyalist slaves and his secret silver mine, which has not been discovered to this day, were stories I asked for again and again.

Along with the normal ailments of the day, such as rheumatism and arthritis, my mother suffered in her later years with a severe form of neuralgia called *tic douloureux*. Without warning her face would crumple with stabbing pains around the nose and mouth, and for a few excruciating minutes she was speechless in agony. Doctors could offer no help except analgesics, which of course never took effect until after the attack. She bore this affliction with great equanimity, claiming it was merely a "cross she had to bear."

Another "cross" was her terror of snakes. It is not easy to live on a large farm in southern Ontario and avoid them. They slithered over rock piles, around fence posts and dropped out of forkfuls of hay with great frequency. Whenever our mother took to the fields, one of our jobs as children was to run ahead in order to assure safe passage.

I would guess that a person, if extremely lucky, can find two or three four-leaf clovers in a lifetime. My mother found hundreds. Even today, when I open any of her poetry books or the old family Bible, they come tumbling out, pressed stiff and brown with age. Long after she had left the farm and moved to a small but comfortable cottage in a nearby town, I questioned her about this ability to spot these elusive plants.

"Well, when most people walk, they look straight ahead. I was always looking down. I wasn't searching for four-leaf clovers, I was keeping an eye out for something else. Like Santayana, 'I like to walk about amidst the beautiful things that adorn the world.' I never thought that should include snakes."

TRAVELLING

Modern modes of travel and a higher standard of living have allowed many of us to visit places our parents and grandparents only dreamed about.

Complaining about the drinking water in Mexico or the narrow roads in Katmandu is the stuff of cocktail party chatter. Those marvellous slides of Mount Kilimanjaro taken from your hotel balcony are filed quickly away to make room for the new ones of Hawaii.

My mother loved faraway places but only knew them through books, songs and poetry. Through my television work I have travelled to many countries over the years and met many interesting people, but I believe my mother would have relished and appreciated these experiences more. She was born to travel and never did.

I have found myself on a span over the Tiber in Rome wondering what she would have made of standing where "Horatio kept the Bridge" or while sightseeing in Scotland recalling how she sang the praises of "Bonnie Doon" and the "Scots wha hae wi Wallace bled." Victor Hugo's "Les Contemplations" would make

Paris seem a much different city to her than my *Michelin Guide* ever could to me.

I was able to take her on a vacation only once. It was in the 1950s and I had my first "holiday with pay" from a radio station in St. Catharines. This meant sixty-five dollars free and clear with two weeks in which to spend it. I borrowed a car and drove to Trenton, where I convinced my mother to take a few days' holiday.

Neither of us had seen the Parliament Buildings, so off we went down Highway Seven to Ottawa. Though she was in her seventies, she ran me ragged, scampering around the government buildings, watching coins being made at the mint, posing with scarlet-coated Mounties and inspecting for hours each item on display in the museum and art gallery. After two days I was ready to come home.

We headed back to Trenton by way of Number Two Highway, stopping at Fort Henry and indulging ourselves in a Thousand Islands boat tour. On the outskirts of Kingston, my mother's sharp eyes spotted a small sign that read Abbey Dawn.

"Do you suppose Wallace Havelock Robb might be home?" she wondered. Robb had been a favourite new poet for some time. His column and nature musings appeared regularly in one of the farm papers and we had a few of his books of verse.

Not only was he home, but he welcomed us with great panache. When he found out my mother could recite some of his poems from memory, he demanded that she ring Gitchi Nagamo, his giant, six-hundred-pound bronze poet's bell. He gave her a personal tour of his native museum and insisted she try on Bliss Carmen's old black hat, which had been entrusted to him by Canada's poet laureate. Later, in front of his massive fireplace, wearing his stately poet's robes, he "performed" several of his more epic works for his enthralled and delighted visitor.

In the years that followed, I got to know Wallace Havelock Robb and his family quite well and produced a radio documentary about him for the CBC. Up until his death in 1976, he kept in touch by sending me notes, cards and snatches of poetry from time to time. He always remembered my mother and until she died in 1969 sent her a letter and a poem every Christmas.

My mother never got to visit Shakespeare's Stratford-on-Avon or Thoreau's Walden Pond, but she did get to Abbey Dawn and meet one of her favourite poets whose kindness and generous spirit made her one and only vacation a memorable one.

September

September

Harvest time involved everyone in the family plus neighbours. Although we had our own binder and corn harvester, we depended on the man with the threshing machine and the silo filler to do the final jobs with the help of twenty or so of our friends. It seemed as if our whole spring and summer labours were crammed into three frantic days as teams of horses hauled huge wagonloads of grain in a continuing stream to feed the thresher. As I grew older, my part in the harvest operation changed as I took on greater responsibility. When I was five or six, my job was to carry buckets of cold water to the men in the fields. Running from wagon to wagon, I would watch in amazement the amount of water they could gulp down parched throats and willingly oblige when asked to pour a dipper-full over their sweaty heads. At ten or twelve, I was driving the horses, moving carefully from stook to stook, sometimes barely pausing as the sheaves came flying up on the wagon to be stacked in precise rows for transport to the barn. Then, in my teens, I became one of "the men." Either in the field, pitching the sheaves onto the wagons, or at the barn as a "spike" pitcher, where I mounted each loaded wagon in turn and fed the hungry maw of the giant threshing machine, the pace was frantic and continuous.

I remember when the thresher was powered by a huge steam engine with its boiler fired by wood. This iron monster would spew smoke and steam as the giant pulley wheel turned the belt to the thresher. Later, of course, the tractor took over and would run for hours, its steel-lugged wheels braced with wooden blocks to keep the belt taut and the pulleys turning.

As the grain entered the thresher, slashing knives cut the twine that bound the sheaves, then they disappeared into a drum-like interior to be tumbled and blown apart. A paddle-wheel apparatus shot the straw with incredible pressure up the blower onto an ever-mounting golden pile, while the kernels of grain were driven down a pipe into a bagger that held and filled two hemp sacks at once. Sometimes I worked the bagger and learned to quickly tie that special farmer's knot that keeps the load secure while you hoist it on your shoulder, run to the granary, dump it and return before the second bag starts to overflow.

There were no baggers involved with corn. Everything was chopped, leaves, cobs, stalks alike, and blown up the long pipe that led to the top of the silo. The silage then fell some sixty feet through the air to land in a dusty pile that had to be pitched flat and tramped down by foot. This was considered the worst job of all. To spend a day in the enclosed silo, blinded by chaff, unable to breathe without a damp handkerchief tied over the mouth, pitching and tramping while hard bullets of corn and stalks fell on your head and shoulders was not a pleasant chore. Old-timers who had filled many silos in their time were keen on offering advice to teenagers.

"There's only one way to survive in there, Roy; you have to have a chew."

Then they would hand me a plug of tobacco and tell me to bite off a chunk.

"It will keep your head clear and your throat lubricated. Just don't forget to spit."

It actually worked well until that moment when a large cob of corn hit you on the head and you swallowed the entire cud. From then on your job became no easier as with heaving stomach you slowly turned as green as the silage beneath your feet.

The best part of the threshing and silo-filling days was mealtime. The farm women in the area joined forces to load their great pine kitchen tables with platters of food until they fairly groaned. Large joints of beef, ham or roast pork, bowls of mashed potatoes, turnips and squash, rich gravy, home-made bread and butter, cabbage or jellied salads made up the first course. Just when you thought you couldn't hold another crumb, in would come at least three kinds of pie. Apple, pumpkin and raspberry were perennial favourites, but frequently a specialty of the house, such as lemon meringue or chocolate with shredded coconut, would be added to the dessert list. And always, some shy but proud member of the host family would venture, "I do hope you can make out a meal."

It was community involvement at its highest level. No one farm family could have managed it alone. The sharing of horses, wagons, muscle and food brought our daily existence to a near spiritual level. Neighbours with disagreements at other months of the year came together through mutual necessity to work shoulder to shoulder during harvest time.

Perhaps more than anything else, it is this spirit of lending a helping hand, this joy of leaning on each other that I miss in today's society.

THE HICKORY HARVEST

"The autumn weather turns the leaves to flame, / And we haven't got time for the waiting game."

"September Song" was written by Kurt Weill for the musical *Knicker-bocker Holiday*. The actor Walter Huston, who couldn't sing a note, recorded it in recitation fashion with a lush orchestral backing and it became an immediate hit in 1938.

Whenever I hear it, I remember that year and I remember the day we gathered the hickory nuts.

Two giant hickories stood within squirrel-hopping distance from each other in the centre of a twenty-acre grain field just south of the railway tracks on our family farm. Each year they provided us with our winter supply of this versatile and uniquely delicious food.

Compared to hickory nuts, walnuts are bland and bitter, peanuts are heavy and oily, cashews are – well, just cashews. Hickory nuts are light, crisp, smoky-sweet and extremely hard to crack. Long before nuts came vacuum-packed, cellophane-wrapped and salted to within an inch of their flavour, the hickory nut was inspiring country cuisine. They were liberally tossed into cakes and muffins, folded into candy and sprinkled on desserts of every kind. I enjoyed eating them straight from the shell. This required a hammer and either an anvil or flat rock, or, when indoors, the bottom of my mother's flat iron.

The fall of 1938 was a good year for most crops in this area, but no one had ever seen our hickory trees so loaded. Every inch of the huge branches seemed to be covered with flat, dark husks, and we would have to hurry to rescue them from the squirrels, chipmunks and raccoons. Working days were too full of threshing, silo-filling and fall ploughing to do anything as frivolous as gathering nuts, so this left only Sunday.

My parents were against working on the Sabbath beyond what was absolutely necessary, but they were also against facing a long winter with no treats. Besides, this could hardly be considered work.

After the morning chores and breakfast, my two older brothers and I drove the mare and democrat down to the trees and began stuffing the nuts into bran sacks in preparation for drying on the barn floor. Our parents soon joined us along with an older sister who had just popped in from across the bay.

We never actually stopped for lunch. Someone brought a loaf of home-made bread and cheese from the house. We opened a jug of fresh apple cider and ate as we worked. Two teen-aged cousins arrived to show off their new girlfriends and all four soon decided picking hickory nuts was a lot of fun. A couple of bachelor neighbours arrived with a jug of cider that wasn't quite as new and a complete stranger, who had been riding the rails, hopped off a passing boxcar to give us a hand. The minister and his wife stopped by to see us and decided to stay.

By four o'clock, there must have been twenty-five people of all ages there. Some were up the trees shaking the limbs, showering nuts on those below who were filling the bags for others to dump in the democrat to be driven and unloaded in the barn. One after another would start a song, some the latest from the hit parade, some as old as the trees we harvested, and everyone would join in. Much to the embarrassment but secret mirth of my mother, the minister decided that the words to "Bringing in the Sheaves" could just as well be changed to "Bringing in the Nuts."

The day wore on, the fun and laughter continuing, and when it was finally decided that the squirrels were welcome to what was left, we all trooped up to the farmhouse. Bushels of sweet corn were husked and roasted, platters of potato salad with hard-boiled eggs were passed around and fresh sun-ripened watermelons were sliced into juicy chunks. No one seemed to want to leave. My brother brought out his harmonica and banjo and as the sky turned red, then purple and finally grey, we sang and laughed and watched our whole world change.

For change it did! I never saw many of those people again. Crops in the 1930s weren't always bountiful. Some neighbours gave up and moved away. Some of the laughing teenagers volunteered and marched off to war the following year. Some of them never came back. I had to leave and go to a distant school. The following September, in a violent storm, a bolt of lightning shattered both the old hickory trees and turned them into blackened stumps.

Now and again I have thought of the day and marvelled at our innocence. A few years ago, my oldest sister died. Toward the end, she seldom recognized visitors to her hospital room. After sitting with her in silence one afternoon and thinking she had fallen asleep, I was starting to leave when I saw her lips move. I leaned closer over the bed. There was a faint smile and I heard her whisper, "I was just remembering the day we gathered the hickory nuts."

The end of summer and the completion of the harvest brought a collective sigh of relief to all who made their living by farming. Whatever had been dug, reaped, picked or piled in these last few days was evidence of the success or failure of the preceding months of toil. All that remained was to turn over the acres of sod and stubble with ploughshares and disk to prepare the land for winter's nurture.

This was not a job for children. Arrow-straight furrows with matching crests and headlands so uniform they framed the field in geometric precision could not be executed by a day-dreaming boy who would just be "in the way." Far better to cut off his summer growth of hair, make sure his ears were washed and send him off for "learnin'."

THE FIRST DAY OF SCHOOL

Along with thousands of Canadian children my oldest granddaughter, Jessie, starts her first day of school on Tuesday — the first day of a probable stretch of over five thousand days in the classroom.

I expect she will be delighted with her experience on Tuesday and that her enthusiasm will continue unabated. For that reason I have never told her about my first day at school. This is unusual for us, because Jessie and I have shared many a laugh when answering her perennial question, "What was it like when you were my age, Grandpa?"

My first day of school was no laughing matter. It was 1936 and the Ontario Ministry of Education had just brought in "The New Course of Study." Gone were the old divisions of senior and junior classes where you started elementary school in "junior first" and graduated from "senior fourth." It had become just grades one through eight. Kindergarten hadn't found its way into the rural system yet. Gone too were the old, dull readers that my older brothers and sisters had struggled with for years. I was to begin with a spanking new, bright blue primer with coloured pictures and crisp text describing the exploits of *Mary, John and Peter*. It was the first year everything was free. Pencils, erasers, scribblers, rulers and art paper were all provided by the school, to the relief of depression-strapped parents.

I already knew my alphabet and numbers, could identify most words in books and recite several lengthy poems even before that first day. The prospect of learning more and the thrill of this new adventure had me fairly bursting with excitement.

There were seven of us in grade one taking up an entire row in the small room that held all eight grades. The teacher was new to everyone.

Miss Bone was tall, plump and wore a dark green dress buttoned high around her neckline like a tunic. That green dress and a navy blue one of the same cut were the only two I was ever to see her wear.

"My name is Miss Bone. I'm your new teacher," she said. "I want the grade one class to come up and form a line here at the front." We all skipped forward eagerly.

She took from her desk a wide, stiff strap about two feet long. "Put out your hands," she said. We did as we were told. She then went down the line and strapped all of us four times on each hand.

I burst into tears. Little Benny Marsden peed his pants. The others were crying too, even some of the older students who were sitting in shock and disbelief. Through the sounds of sobbing I heard Miss Bone say, "This is to get you started out on the right foot. There will be no acting up in my school. You will do your work and pay attention. Always remember this day!"

I certainly never forgot. But not in the way she intended. I saw it as a mean, frightening thing she had done. No one had ever struck me before. My parents had never hit or spanked me. I didn't know adults did that kind of thing. I hated her for many years.

Later on, I met other kinds of teachers. Men and women who smiled and laughed with me, cared about me, loved me and fanned that desire to learn back to the flame it had once been.

I have had the good fortune to meet thousands of teachers across Canada in classrooms, conventions and professional development seminars. I am proud and delighted with their dedication to the students of this country. I am, however, saddened to learn that corporal punishment is still allowed by some school boards. A principal in Alberta told me last year, "It says a lot about our society that I am legally empowered to take a strap and hit a child but, if I put my arms around one of them or give them an affectionate kiss, I can be brought into court for child molestation."

Good luck, Jessie! I'm sure you'll do fine. But if anyone ever reaches for a strap, tell them you've got a real tough Grandpa with a very long memory.

Over the years I feel I have received a good education, but I am not what we used to call "well schooled." As a matter of fact I am what is commonly known as a high school drop-out.

The primary or public schools of rural Ontario in the thirties were designed to teach the farmers' offspring to read, write and "figure." There was no expectation or encouragement toward higher learning. The eight years spent in these one-room brick buildings were in preparation for a life on the family farm until, reaching the age of sexual maturity, you married a neighbour girl and worked one or the other of the parents' farms on shares. The family home was then divided or the tenant house re-modelled in preparation for a new brood of children to continue this rarely broken cycle. Not much "book learnin'" was needed to milk cows, shovel manure or hoe turnips and even less to have children.

This attitude toward education was persistent in local school boards, obvious in teacher selection and heartily endorsed by parents who anxiously awaited their sons' and daughters' return to the work-force.

The teacher, always a woman, usually boarded at a nearby farm home and often lacked her high school diploma, considered a minimum requirement for city school teaching. The provincial department of education sent around an inspector once a year who would sit at the back of the room while the nervous teacher asked the brighter kids to read out loud or do their multiplication tables on the black-board. In all my time in public school the same man came and he always stood up just before he left and told us the same story. It was about a little rabbit that got a stone caught in its teeth, couldn't eat and died of starvation. I heard the story seven times and could never figure out whether the moral was always to brush our teeth or not to eat stones.

The reason I didn't hear it eight times was because a miracle happened in grade seven. Our new teacher that year was married, drove her car in every day from the city, wore red lipstick and nail polish, loved teaching and told me I was bright. She insisted on driving me home one day to meet my parents. No teacher had ever entered our house before and I'm sure my father thought I'd been caught in some despicable act.

"Roy is wasting his time in this school. I want your permission to combine his grade seven and eight so he can take his entrance exams and start high school this fall."

It was likely at that moment my parents knew they had lost a farm-hand.

There was no way I could have stayed home and gone to high school. Unlike today, we did not have the big yellow buses that cruise the country roads and, like giant vacuum cleaners, suck up kids at every mailbox to deposit them in city learning facilities. The other problem was financial. My family would be very hard pressed to find money for text-books and proper school clothes, let alone room and board. My older sister Clara and her husband Ed came to my rescue. They lived in the town of Stirling about forty miles north of Trenton, where a small high school served a wide area of Hastings County. Despite having five small children, very little income and cramped living space, they welcomed me into their home.

The day before school opened, my Dad sold a pig and with the twenty dollars he received took me into Bob Patterson's Dry Goods Store in Stirling. He picked out a brown tweed suit, a pair of black shoes and a white shirt for the money and Mr. Patterson insisted on throwing in a bright orange tie. Ed trimmed my hair with the kitchen scissors.

The next day in the grade nine classroom,

with the other boys in their casual sweaters, open-necked coloured shirts and sports jackets, it was easy to spot the kid from the farm.

I liked school. A whole new realm of subjects was opened to me. Scientific experiments with real Bunsen burners and Petri dishes, painting and drawing with oils and India ink, Shakespeare's plays and sonnets, Spinoza's theories and Leacock's humour. I liked the town. I enjoyed walking on pavement to the theatre that showed movies Friday and Saturday nights, to Whitehead's Cafe where all the kids my age hung out after school and to the public library where I spent many happy hours for the next year and a half. I had never in my life seen that many books in one place and my ten-cent library card gave me access to all of them.

I have, over the years, been in some of the finest libraries in the world and I have seen private collections that would make the Stirling offering seem meagre, but I will always have a fond memory of that small brick building that opened so many wonderful doors for me.

The months passed quickly. I helped my sister as much as I could by baby-sitting and doing chores around her busy house. Her older two children had started school and enjoyed having their uncle "who went to high school" drop them off each morning. On Saturdays I was able to get a job with a local contractor and with a shovel and a bucket cleaned out septic tanks for three dollars and fifty cents a day. I also cut lawns in the evening and hoed cabbages for a local market gardener. Any extra money I could make went for school supplies, clothes and sometimes to help with the groceries.

In March of 1945, in the middle of my grade ten year, an older brother died unexpectedly. He had contracted pneumonia after being gored by a bull. I got the news in the library. My six-year-old nephew raced in and announced loudly, "Mom says you have to come home; she has some bad news to tell you. She also says you won't be living with us any more." He was right on both counts.

Two of my brothers had married sisters and ran a big dairy farm on the shores of Lake Erie, near Long Beach. Now, with one dead, the other needed help and came up with a plan that involved me. I was of course to attend the funeral but, instead of returning with the rest of the family, I would stay and transfer to Port Colborne High School. I would also work on the farm to pay for my keep.

The plan was for me to drive the milk route, which entailed loading our own cans on the truck in the morning, picking up the overnight supply from about a dozen other farms, unloading them at the dairy in Port Colborne, then proceeding on to school. After four o'clock, the ritual would be reversed as I picked up the cleaned cans and delivered them back to the farms. On top of this I had morning and evening chores seven days a week, plus all day on Saturdays. Gone was any chance to read for pleasure or even keep up with regular schoolwork.

On top of this was a strange school principal who objected to having area farm kids included in his jurisdiction and refused to show any consideration for their needs. Being only fifteen, I had to be issued a special driver's licence in order to operate the truck. The principal didn't like seeing his students behind the wheel of a vehicle, so he banned me from parking on school property. He also insisted that all his farm students take part in Army Cadets. This was an extra-curricular activity involving uniforms, twenty-two calibre rifles and marching. That was his idea of preparing us for active service. Even though VE day was joyously celebrated on May 8th that year, our principal had no intention of allowing his grade ten students to lay down their arms. From four until six o'clock we ran around the school track in full uniform and pack, presented and shouldered arms, marched and got screamed at until, finally released, we started the long journey home where we were screamed at again for delaying chores.

I was lonely and unhappy. I had no time or place to study and was getting no encouragement in or out of school. I barely made it into grade eleven.

One Saturday in October, when I was sixteen, stands out as a turning-point in my life. It was a beautifully warm day and I was told to pick the plums which hung so heavily that the branches nearly touched the ground. There would be dozens of bushels to ship to a processor in Welland. My brother would be in town all day on business.

Unfortunately, the corn was also ripe and the cows knew it. They spent most of their day knocking down the fence to get into the corn field and I spent an equal amount of time chasing them out and repairing the damage. Finally, in desperation, I drove them into the barn and locked the door. I was high atop the ladder filling my first bushel of plums when my brother came home.

"Why are the cows in the barn?"

"They've been jumping the fence and getting into the corn."

"Why didn't you fix the fence?"

"I did. They knocked it down again."

"Where are the rest of the plums?"

"This is all I have picked."

"You've been here all day and you've only picked one bushel! What am I to do with one bushel of plums?"

I took a deep breath, climbed down the ladder, looked him straight in the eye and told him exactly what he could do with his bushel of plums... one by one.

I walked out of the orchard, past the house, down the side-road to the main highway and kept walking. My days of working on someone else's farm were over. So were my days of school.

I have been very involved with the education system of this country at all levels. I have worked with teachers in seminars, started schools, served on boards of governors and written textbooks for grades I never reached. I have been honoured with six honorary doctorates from universities across Canada and met thousands of students at dozens of convocations. I have no regrets and yet sometimes I wonder what it would have been like to have gone on to higher learning.

Often in the fall, when I'm visiting some campus for a speaking engagement or a film assignment, the desire wafts over me like some half-remembered dream. When I see laughing students rushing to classes, scattering flaming leaves in their path, their arms full of books, their sweaters emblazoned with team names or scholastic honours, their voices eager and full of humour, their eyes bright with expectation, I feel a pang of having missed a very special part of life. Then again, maybe it's just that time of year.

October

October

Around this time of year many people say goodbye to their summer cottages having packed away the boat, shuttered the windows and disconnected the water-pipes. Memories of family barbecues, beach parties and loon cries are carried back to the city to be pleasantly savoured during our long Canadian winters.

Some friends of ours go even farther. They transfer their bathing suits, sun block and flip-flops to the trunk of their cars and head for Florida. It seems that at the first honk of a south-bound Canada goose, they fear the icy blasts of winter are upon them. These "snowbirds," as they have been dubbed, miss the glories of our most beautiful month.

I can't imagine exchanging the brilliant panoply of maple, oak and sumac for the wonders of Disney World or Cape Canaveral. Even if these attractions had been around when I was a boy, I'm sure I would still have opted for this month's simple joys.

I spend a lot of time in the woods in October. My woodlot is at the very rear of the farm and includes a variety of trees that form a nearly impenetrable fortress protecting wildlife of all descriptions. Sometimes I feel like an intruder on my own property as the animals and birds watch with puzzled curiosity my stroll through their environs. I usually carry a can of paint to daub the trunks of leafless and dying trees so they can be spotted later when the woods are full of snow. These trees will be felled, cut and split for firewood. It is also a good time to pick out the Christmas tree.

When we first moved to the farm, we noticed about an acre of white pine saplings that had sprung up following some slash-cutting by a previous owner. Over the years, we have selected one each Christmas to be brought to the house for decoration. The remaining trees have grown into a dense grove of towering pine with intermingling branches that form a cathedral-like ceiling, shutting out the sun, wind and snow. The earth beneath these branches is thick with old pine needles that spring back in place leaving no tracks as you walk through. When you sit quietly on this soft, brown carpet, squirrels, jackrabbits, chipmunks, even mice, creep close to cock a quizzical eye in your direction. On the pine limbs high above, finches and cardinals interrupt the chattering jays to fill the scene with music. What a privilege it is to sit here and be part of a world that makes no demand on you except to be respected and cherished.

Out in the deciduous part of the woods, through the stands of oak, ash, maple and birch, run the trails made by deer, fox and wolf. Some years, when weather conditions have caused meagre foraging in northern areas, bear tracks and droppings are seen. Wild turkeys, pheasants and grouse explode with a flurry of beating wings from stands of juniper or prickly ash. Now and again, hunters find the temptation too hard to resist.

Remnants of an old wooden fence separating my property from my neighbour's are an attractive but ineffective barrier to anyone wanting access to the woods. These long, cedar rails were split and shaped by native Mohawks near Tyendinaga who supplied them to the early homesteaders in the late 1700s. They are moss-covered and grey with age but still strong and seemingly indestructible. The cedar rail fences of rural Ontario are gradually disappearing as hunters, snowmobilers, campers and weekend tourists find them irresistible as lawn decorations, patio dividers or fireplace kindling. The ones that are left are certainly no defence against the October "sportsmen."

With the opening of the hunting season, I can always expect a crimson-clad, shotgun-toting visitor at my door. The conversation usually goes something like this.

"Is that your property back there north of the creek on the west side of the road?"

"Yes, it is."

"I noticed a couple of nice looking buck at the edge of the woods. Thought I might try my luck if you don't mind."

"As a matter of fact, I do mind. You see, I don't allow hunting on my property so that's why the animals like coming here. They know they're safe."

"You're one of those anti-hunting people, are you?"

"Yes and no. I feel that if a person needs the food to keep from starving, hunting is justified. I feel that if wolves are attacking and killing livestock they have to be stopped. If gophers are destroying my vegetables or raccoons are stripping my corn field, steps have to be taken to prevent it. But I don't believe in shooting animals for fun."

"Well, I just thought I'd ask. If I don't shoot them, some other hunter will."

"I'm very pleased you asked. I appreciate the courtesy. I might point out that I am quite able to hear any shot that is fired in my woods. I can have the provincial police here faster than any hunter can drag his kill back out to the road. Have a good day."

One animal that a lot of farmers would like to see eliminated is the beaver. This Canadian national emblem spends most of its time damming creeks, flooding pastures, chewing down valuable trees and blocking waterways needed for thirsty stock and parched crops. My family of beavers is a little more discerning. They have taken up residence in a section of my creek that runs through an unused field of scrub and swamp. October is the perfect time to wander back, find a comfortable log and watch these buck-toothed rodents perform their engineering feats.

With incredible energy they construct their lodges in the shape of a dome, using sticks and mud. One or two tunnels lead into the creek bank or through long canals to other auxiliary lodges. Branches, twigs and even small logs are anchored in the mud below the ice line where the weather is deepest, to provide a submerged storage area for winter food. The whole family works. While the mates are gnawing through trees up to two feet in width, the kips are swimming across the small lake they've created, towing branches and roots, slapping mud with their flat tails and looking up at me now and again to see if I approve. While beavers can be a real pest in many rural areas, they are doing no harm on my farm. Once their pond has frozen over, my grandchildren enjoy it as a large, unobstructed skating rink. I often wonder if down below the ice in their watery, winter retreat the beaver family knows what joy they have brought to the kids who are frolicking above, to say nothing of the pleasure they gave me as I watched them back in October.

WATERMELONS

October always reminds me of my past life in organized crime. I was part of a gang that robbed and pillaged during the 1940s.

As the leaves turned to gold and the air developed that "see-your-breath" nip, a group of us farm kids would meet in the autumnal darkness a couple of nights a week to steal our neighbours' watermelons. It was a ritual passed on from one generation to the next and was as much a part of growing up in rural Ontario as smoking corn silk or chewing slippery elm. Crawling on your stomach in the chilly dark, under rail fences and through wet vines, may not seem terribly exciting to the youth of today, but it beats watching TV re-runs or hanging around shopping malls.

In groups of four or five we would feel our way along the rows, sharply tapping the melons until we found a couple with the hollow echo that meant perfect ripeness. Scampering back to our pre-arranged hide-out, we'd meet our partners in crime, slice up our loot by lantern shine and spend half the night slurping juice, spitting seeds and bragging about how clever we were. Even the knowl-edge that all the farmers, including our own parents, planted extra rows every year just for us to steal didn't diminish the thrill. All the farmers, that is, except Sam Christie.

An unfortunate incident before our time prevented him from looking kindly on our midnight maraudings. One fall our older brothers and sisters had mistakenly made off with the prize melon he had been care-fully nurturing to exhibit at the Belleville Fair. He had pampered this beautiful specimen with high-potency fertilizer and bacterial inoculants (a garden variety of athletes' steroids) for several months until it weighed almost fifty pounds.

After it disappeared, he even put

ads in the local papers that read, "A reward is offered for information leading to the apprehension, etc.," but there was honour among those thieves. Nobody squealed. The next year he bought guard dogs and electric fences for his patch and my friends and I had to live with our older siblings' error. Sam Christie also put an end to the other October crime in which I was involved.

There was no such thing as "trick or treat" at Hallowe'en. There were just tricks. In the country this meant knocking over outhouses. About five by five by eight feet, sturdily constructed with shingled roofs, papered on the inside with newspapers to prevent draughts, they proudly sat thirty to forty feet away from the farmhouse over a deep pit. Most were two-holers, one slightly smaller with a step up for tiny bottoms.

Every farmer knew that part of Hallowe'en was re-erecting his outhouse the morning after. Every farmer, that is, except Mr. Christie. He wanted no part of these shenanigans and took extreme measures to keep his privy upright

Our intrepid gang had been outwitted by Mr. Christie for the past two years. One Hallowe'en, he fastened his outhouse to the clothes-line and as a further precaution hung sleigh bells on the line. Not only did it fail to topple, but he was on the scene chasing us at the sound of the first jingle. The next year, he actually sat inside it, emerging with a shotgun loaded with rock salt when he heard our stealthy approach.

This year we were determined. Eight of us plotted and planned for days, finally coming up with what we thought was a foolproof strategy. We would sneak as close as we dared to the door side and then, at a signal from our leader, we would rush the building, hitting it hard like a surprise military raid, then keep on running. If it was fastened to the clothes-line, our combined weight would surely knock it loose and if he was sitting inside, well, so be it. Since I had initially suggested the plan, I was chosen leader.

We waited patiently until the moon slid behind a cloud, then crept quietly around the side of the farmhouse. We had correctly guessed his dogs would be down in the field guarding the melon patch. A whispered check assured me that my fellow commandos were in place. I took a deep breath, yelled "ATTACK" and we all surged toward the little building and our ignoble defeat.

Mr. Christie had simply moved his outhouse five feet back. Half of us ended up in the pit, buried to our hips. The other half pulled us out and spent the rest of the night sloshing us down with pails of water and carbolic soap.

Now and again, when a youngster comes to my door on Hallowe'en and sings out, "Trick or treat?" I'm tempted to ask, "How about a trick?" Then, I reason, why encourage a new generation to follow in my criminal ways?

For the most part, country people are not law-breakers. They tend to do the right thing, pay their bills and mind their own business. It's true that with careful figuring some income tax can often be avoided; subsidies for not growing certain crops are handy; gasoline tax rebates, even though used in the family car, are accepted; and a few other minor infractions are committed which might be construed as dishonest by some city folk. The fact is that today, as it was in the 1930s, any time you can make an extra buck on the farm is a real accomplishment.

The family farm as I knew it is impossible to run today. The initial cost of land and machinery, the high overhead and maintenance expense coupled with the embarrassingly low price paid for produce keep today's farmer constantly teetering on the brink of bankruptcy. Where we made most of our money from milk and some from pigs or vegetables, today we would have a milk contract worth hundreds of thousands of dollars, raise enough pork to be eligible for membership in the hog marketing board and have our land taken over by a multinational food processor for the harvesting and packaging of our vegetables. And we wouldn't be much further ahead.

When the farm fails, its more than just another business going under. It's a way of life disappearing and a proud tradition that once built and sustained this country ending. When today's young farmers lose the land to the bank, there's a feeling that past generations of family are heaping on loads of guilt and shame. After all, for two hundred years through good times and bad, flood and drought, war and depression, these acres were preserved for them; now they will be dug up for subdivision or paved over for a shopping mall. No wonder suicide statistics are climbing so rapidly in today's rural communities.

Most farmers I know realize they have chosen a tough life. They don't want any consideration they are not entitled to have. They do want a fair price for their produce and some understanding of the problems they face in an increasingly urban society. They also love what they're doing.

At the end of the day, sinking finally onto the porch swing, feeling the breeze drift in off the freshly cut alfalfa and listening to the radio as some guy in a helicopter tells you how the city streets are snarled with exhaust-spewing traffic, the farmer smiles and counts his blessings.

HELPING THEMSELVES

William Cullen Bryant called autumn, "the melancholy days," "the saddest of the year." I find the fall, especially October, a rich and glorious time of lush harvests and vibrant colours.

Living in the country is a real plus at this time of year. The cool misty mornings demand a sweater for that early trip to the barn and far pastures are smoky blue when the orange sun sets. Cars from the city crunch their way along the gravel roads while the passengers soak up the colours and smells of rural Ontario.

Most visitors from town are welcome but there is one breed of urbanite who shouldn't be allowed beyond pavement. He is the "Let's-drive-out-to-the-country-and-get-something-for-nothing" bum. In the fall, farmers become accustomed to city families dropping off their unwanted (and usually pregnant) cats and dogs within walking distance of our warm barns. We are familiar with the used mattresses, rusting bed springs and broken lawn ornaments festooning the ditches of our concession roads. But we find thieves even more difficult to excuse.

Apples and sweet corn are the big

targets in October. Weekends at dusk are the favourite times. Very often it's a family outing and the children are sent scampering into the fields to bring back bags of produce while the parents wait in the car.

Since I don't grow acres of fruit or vegetables, I was surprised on a visit to my "back forty" to see a car parked along the road and a family group in my "spring field," a few acres of bush and trees. As I came closer I saw they were equipped with shovels and were digging out saplings and young evergreen shrubs.

"What's going on?" I asked.

"Oh, hi! We've just moved into a new subdivision. There are no trees or bushes, so we're going to take these back and plant them in our yard."

"But they're mine!"

"Well, you've got lots of them for heaven's sake. You won't miss these."

"That's not the point. This is my property."

"I don't see a sign."

"I shouldn't have to put up a sign saying, 'Don't Steal My Trees!'"

The mother and father looked at me as if I was the biggest grouch in Hastings County. The children hung their heads.

"If you had stopped by the house, I would have been happy to let you have some. As it is, there's no way you can really put them back, so take them home, plant them and at least your children will have a constant reminder over the years of what thieves their parents are."

The loss of a few shrubs is no big deal for me, but the loss of farmers' crops, a bushel here, a bushel there, can add up to significant drain on an income that already shows the slimmest profit margin in our society.

This past week, I noticed a family in a station wagon drive past the house and slowly turn down the side-road hidden by the high corn in my neighbour's fields on either side of the road. The evening breeze brought the sounds of excited voices and I could see the tops of the corn stalks breaking as ears were being ripped off. A short time later there was a slamming of doors and a spewing of gravel as the car sped off.

Why didn't I yell at them to GET OUT? Why didn't I call the police or at least my neighbour to report these metropolitan miscreants? Because they were stealing Bishop 30-28, known by farmers between Kingston and Oshawa as the most hardy hybrid variety of silage corn. Sometimes called "hard corn" or "cow corn," these lovely fat cobs look scrumptious, but no amount of boiling will change them from tasteless, tooth-cracking bullets of fodder. *Bon appetit.* Score one for our side.

November

November

Our old farm community looked after itself. We seldom had to go to the specialists for help or advice. Medical requirements for human or animal were mostly attended to by old remedies that had been passed down for generations. Very often the nostrum was the same for both.

I had the usual childhood diseases and was fortunate enough not to contact those for which serum had yet to be discovered. For simple ailments, there was always something on hand to ease the pain. A clove bud stuck in a cavity eased a toothache. An earache felt better when you held a bag of heated salt against it. A warm, wet tea bag fastened to your eye overnight made a sty disappear by morning and left your sheets full of tea leaves. A silk stocking around your throat when it was sore, turpentine and brown sugar for worms, iodine for cuts, boracic acid for disinfectant and carbolic soap, if lice were suspected, were routine treatments.

Colds were inevitable for every member of the family. Working in all kinds of weather, freezing in some rooms of the house, roasting in others and sleeping two and three to a bed, meant someone was always sneezing or coughing at any given time.

DESERONTO PUBLIC LIBRARY

Fortunately catnip or peppermint tea would make you sleep, honey and eucalyptus would soothe the throat and a sniff from a strange brown bottle on the sideboard would clear out the most stubborn nasal passages. It was many years before I found out it was nothing but a bottle of stale horse urine and it was the ammonia fumes that did the job.

I have an old recipe book that belonged to my great Aunt Emma and that contains directions for everything from floor paint to wedding cake. One is simply titled "Good Cough Mixture":

> 2 oz glycerine
> 1/2 oz virgin oil of pine
> 8 oz pure whiskey

Doctors or nurses were called only in extreme emergencies or when death seemed inevitable. Social workers didn't exist and ministers were there to preach sermons, not dispense advice or counsel.

This independent way of life existed partly through necessity but I suspect mainly by choice. The community, with its deep Loyalist roots, had a fierce stoicism and took deep pride in looking after its own. To turn over one's affairs or problems to some outside agency was seldom, if ever, contemplated. This was also true in the political arena. It would never occur to anyone to call their member of parliament to solve a problem or extend a favour. After all, he was just one of the neighbours from the area and besides, being home only on weekends, he should be spending his time with his family.

Without intense mass media coverage, local

politicians were not the stars they are today. They were ordinary people who did what they could for their constituents, which wasn't really very much, given the fact everyone fairly well looked after themselves.

POLITICS

There was a time when voting was not so much a decision as a custom. Everyone voted the way their parents and grandparents had voted for years. Where I grew up in the Quinte area, this meant voting Conservative. I was quite surprised when I started school to find out there were other political parties.

Even then it was just a simple choice between Tory and Grit. Oh, there were some people starting a new party out west called the CCF, and we all knew what they were. As for the Grits, they were, we were told, either French or Catholic and likely both. So my family and neighbours voted Conservative every election, no matter who was running.

Actually, you were not "running" for elections in those days. You were "standing." As there was no television, we were spared three-hour debates, mud-slinging commercials and charismatic comparisons. Cam-

DESERONTO PUBLIC LIBRARY

paign advertising amounted to a head and shoulders, column-wide picture of the candidate in the local newspaper with the caption "Re-elect Joe Blow" or "Millard Mossbank Solicits Your Support."

The most effective campaigning was done door-to-door. About a week before the election, the candidates would make their rounds. Dad would meet them at the back door and take them for a walk behind the barn. For a long time I thought my mother was against politicians in the house. Later I realized it was booze she prohibited. Most candidates carried a mickey of rye in their pockets to help sway votes. It may seem rather tacky today, but it was cheaper then establishing federal prisons in the riding.

On election day after the evening chores, you made your way to a nearby farmhouse where the parlour had been temporarily turned into a polling place, put an "X" beside the Tory candidate's name and then spent an hour or two on the verandah complaining with your neighbour about the crops.

The election was never discussed. It wasn't necessary. You knew how everyone else had voted and it wouldn't make much difference anyway since it seemed as though Mackenzie King, "that damned Grit," would be in power forever.

One time in the late 1960s, while I was living in Toronto, I was on a film assignment in Ottawa and staying at the Château Laurier at the same time as the Canadian Radio and Television Commission was holding hearings at the hotel. I was approached by a Belleville businessman who knew that I originally came from the Quinte district. He asked me if I would attend a breakfast meeting he had arranged with his local MP and a couple of the commissioners in the hope I might add some weight to a bit of lobbying he was doing for his broadcasting operation. When he told me his MP was Lee Grills, I agreed. I hadn't seen Mr. Grills for over twenty years. When I knew him, he was the man who came around each fall with his threshing machine to harvest the wheat, oats and barley for the area farmers.

"Well, if it isn't Ben's boy," said Mr. Grills as we started on the eggs benedict in the Château's posh dining lounge. "This is a far cry from some of the farm kitchens we used to eat in, eh? I mind the time your Dad and I ..."

For the next hour he held forth, much to the chagrin of the anxious broadcasters, with stories of threshing and silo-filling, runaway horses, hard cider bouts and tobacco-spitting contests. I enjoyed it thoroughly as he brought back memories of those hard, but simpler times.

As the breakfast meeting broke up at the instigation of our perplexed hosts, Mr. Grills asked, "By the way, did you ever find your shirt?"

"My shirt?"

"Yes. The last time I saw you, you were just a skinny teenager. You had been stook-pitching up at the Curtis place and when we came up for supper your shirt was missing. Every time I see you on television I always wonder if you ever found that shirt!"

Ah, they don't make politicians like that anymore! Or, if they do, I haven't met one lately.

I'm grateful that I've never had to shoulder arms and go to war. I'm a pacifist by inclination and conviction and have always thought there must be a better way to resolve differences than to kill people.

Having said that, I also have the deepest respect and appreciation for those men and women who have offered their services and their lives in the defence of Canada's freedom over the years.

I have spoken to and worked with many

veterans' groups in Canada and been involved in numerous radio and TV shows dealing with defence, peace initiatives and military issues, but there is something about a uniform that makes me nervous and about a gun that makes me want to run instead of march.

I might have gotten it from my father. He thought that joining the army was just another means of collecting unemployment insurance. His theory was that anyone who went into military service was too lazy to hold a regular job. Since this hypothesis extended to anyone who didn't work on a farm, it meant nothing. He never figured out how I could consider talking into a microphone any kind of worthwhile career and always thought that someday I might get a decent job in farming.

My own aversion to things material has more to do with the idea of active combat and the destructive power of armaments. My wife, Jane, and I flew back from Germany once in a Canadian military jet accompanied by the then Chief of Defence General Ramsay Withers. I had been on a speaking tour of Canada's armed forces schools in Lahr and Baden. High over the Atlantic, we talked of crises in the world, Canada's role, and particularly military solutions. He told me, "Your trouble, Roy, is that when you think army, navy or air force, you think war. That is not why we're here. We are here for peace. I am a peace lover, I do not want to fight. It is because I hate war that I have dedicated my life to the armed forces." Because Ramsay Withers was as untypical an army officer as I had ever met, he made a great deal of sense.

I was only nine when the Second World War started. Two of my brothers, Frank and Jack, immediately signed up and spent their early leaves proudly showing off their khakis and blues to admiring relatives and neighbours. I was sometimes given the "privilege" of shining their buttons and badges with Brasso before they returned to camp.

Since Trenton Air Base was the home of the RCAF's largest training command, our town was filled with uniforms and our skies were filled with planes. One summer, our area became famous as the location for the Hollywood movie *Captains of the Clouds*. For a couple of months we watched daily as cameramen, strapped into the open doorways of planes, filmed other aircraft in simulated dog fights over our fields. Some neighbours claimed to have actually seen the stars – James Cagney, Dennis Morgan and Alan Hale – on the streets of Trenton. When the movie finally came to the Trent Theatre, everyone crowded in to see if we could recognize local people or places. The story was about a young American pilot, Cagney, who thinks he is flying into Trenton, New Jersey, and ends up in Canada. He decides while he's here to join the RCAF and despite alienation from everyone around him for most of the picture, turns out to be a loveable hero in the end. Actually it was not a bad picture considering it was designed as a morale booster and a blatant pitch to get the United States into the war.

We were very aware of the war from the American point of view, since the only radio stations available on our old battery-operated Stromberg-Carlson were from Rochester or Syracuse in New York

State. While other Canadians listened to Matthew Halton and Lorne Greene, we hung on every word uttered by Edward R. Murrow and H.V. Kaltenborn. Radio news was very important, since the newspaper was always a day late arriving in our rural mailbox. Letters from my brothers were heavily censored but read and reread by family members and anyone else who came to visit.

Rationing had very little effect on farmers. Though each of us had a ration book filled with stamps, we usually gave them to friends who lived in town. Meat, butter and eggs were obviously no problem for us. With plenty of honey and maple syrup, we didn't need sugar and we wouldn't have burned coal even if we had it. Our main concern was where to get help for planting and harvesting. Farmers were being urged to grow more of all kinds of crops as a patriotic duty. Much was made of the farmerette movement, which offered girls from the city to work side by side with men on the farms. No one in our area thought of that as anything unusual. Our mothers, wives and sisters had been doing that forever.

The months became years and our early excitement and bravado turned to pain as the community shared common grief at funeral services in old White's church. They were almost always the same. An empty casket draped with a red ensign, a military cap and a picture on top, a corps member playing the last post and then we would all sing,

Eternal Father strong to save,
Whose arms doth bind the restless wave

Who bidd'st the mighty ocean deep
Its own appointed limits keep:
O hear us when we cry to thee
For those in peril on the sea.

Some of the deaths occurred on local farms. The RCAF base at Trenton trained thousands of pilots and air crew during the war years and several student flyers crashed in our fields as a result of inexperience or faulty equipment.

One day, we were harvesting pumpkins when we heard the louder than usual roar of a Fleet trainer. It was coming in low over the corn field, so low that the wind was bending the stalks. It cleared the fence directly in front of us but couldn't make it over an old oak tree that had stood for generations at the end of the field. The plane seemed to disintegrate as the huge arms of the tree gathered it in. There was no explosion, just a ripping and splitting of wood and metal, then silence. We rushed forward and watched in horror as parts of the plane and the pilot fell to the ground. It was the first time I had ever seen human death.

The beacon atop the control tower at the Trenton Air Base always sent whirling streams of light into my dark bedroom when I was young. As it swept the room, it illumined the walls and pictures and was a comforting night-light by which to go to sleep. That night I lay awake for a long time as the shafts of light from the beacon seemed to be searching for someone who would never find his way back.

REMEMBRANCE DAY

For a young lad in school, Remembrance Day meant listening to the teacher read John McCrae's "In Flanders Fields" and putting my head down on my desk for the required two-minute silence at eleven o'clock.

Later, as a cub reporter, I covered cenotaph services where the mayor or a local military personage laid wreaths. When in radio, I broadcast these services live, carrying the designated clergyman's homily and the singing of "O God, Our Help in Ages Past" by a scout or guide choir. Then, as guests of the Canadian Legion, we would gather at the local hall, hoist a few beers and listen to the veterans tell war stories – some exciting, some boring. I would join in the beery singing of half-remembered songs and wonder what the day was really about.

In 1971, I was on several film assignments in West Germany, one of which took me to Munich, where preparations were underway for the summer Olympics to be held there the following year. After touring the Olympic site and filming the nearly completed stadium, we were treated

royally by our government hosts —
box seats in the magnificent opera
house, visits to the world famous
breweries and special viewings of the
five hundredth anniversary collection
of Albrecht Dürer paintings. A car
and driver had been put at my dis-
posal during the visit and when I
noticed that Dachau was only a few
miles from Munich, I asked if I could
see the infamous camp located
there. My driver, a Bavarian woman,
who up until then had been most co-
operative, refused. She said that this
was not part of her duties and she
strongly advised any visitors against
going there and dredging up old
memories.

A taxi took me the few miles north-
west of Munich to the small town of
Dachau and deposited me at the
gates of the concentration camp that
had been built in the early thirties on
the former site of an ammunition
factory. The weather had turned cold
and drizzly. A grey mist drifted in
from the nearby Amper River.

As I walked from the gravelled
common area into the cramped
sleeping quarters, I was met with
wall-to-ceiling, life-size photographs
of former inmates. Gaunt faces and
starving bodies seemed to follow me

as I made my way through these dormitories of torture. Some photographs had been taken by their liberators, others by the Nazis who became assiduous in their record-keeping. Over 206,000 prisoners had been held here. More than 32,000 deaths can be certified but thousands more were killed before the official registry was started. Many were sent from Dachau for extermination elsewhere.

From the barracks to the shower stalls that used to spray gas, to the ovens and the burial pits, I followed other stunned and silent tourists. There were only a few of us that dreary day in that desolate place. No one spoke. Some stopped to kneel or bow their heads in the various chapels on the site. Mostly we walked, looked and felt the horror of inhumanity.

The exit from the camp took me along a narrow road past barbed-wire-laden bunkers. I noticed that I was not the only one with tears in my eyes as we gazed at the huge letters on the side of the museum wall that spelled the words, NEVER AGAIN.

Since that experience, Remembrance Day for me has not meant

poppies, cenotaphs or choruses of "Lili Marlene." It has been a day to remember Dachau and a commitment I made there to work for peace and, in whatever way I could, give added hope to those two words.

December

December

I have seven grandchildren under the age of eight and, when they visit, their first stop is a large floor-to-ceiling armoire which is full of games, toys and puzzles. The next is the VCR and television set, where they can choose from a library of movies, cartoons and shows that provide hours of diversion and fun. Never a dull moment.

Compared to today, I suppose we had many a dull moment on the farm, but we never expected the world to provide us with constant amusement. In that time, before "Ninja Turtles," "Ghostbusters" and Trivial Pursuit, fun was home-made and your entertainment depended on your ingenuity.

Of course we had cards, dominoes, checkers, Snakes and Ladders and some jigsaw puzzles, but for the most part our leisure hours were taken up with activities that couldn't be store-bought.

My childhood toys such as swords, bows and arrows and cowboy pistols were carved out of cedar rails by my older brothers. A short-crotched branch and a strip of inner tube made a durable and accurate catapult. Even sleds, hockey sticks and skis were made from used lumber, curved tree limbs or barrel staves. An uncle who had a wood lathe but no knowledge of baseball made us a bat that was so large and heavy I could hardly lift it in my pre-teen years, but when it connected with the ball, it was an automatic home run. A corner of our pasture field made an ideal diamond for many Sunday afternoon games of scrub. This was a version of softball where everyone had a chance to play each position and get a turn at bat. Neighbour kids gravitated to our place for these contests because many of their parents wouldn't allow any games on the Sabbath.

Long winter evenings were spent in a variety of family fun. I was never musically talented but enjoyed singing while Flossie played the piano with Bert on banjo or harmonica and Jack on clarinet. Our music was mostly "by ear" and came from tunes handed down for generations or picked up from the radio. The only record player we had was the old Edison cylinder wind-up model that was long out of date even then. The most recent records we had were by Harry Lauder or John Philip Sousa dated 1910-12. Today this same gramophone, still working, sits in my living room just a few feet from the CD player.

Euchre was a popular rural card game. It was learned at a very early age, since you never knew when you would be called on to make a fourth. Neighbourhood euchre parties were held whenever the snowy roads became passable, and as many as a dozen card tables would be set up throughout the house as entire families from grandpas to babies arrived in cutters and sleighs for an evening of fun and food.

Crokinole was my favourite parlour game. This rural Ontario pastime was played with great seriousness and local champions were held in high regard. A crokinole board has eight sides but is round in the centre, allowing a trough along the edge for spent checkers. It is divided into five-, ten- and fifteen-value-point sections with a twenty-score hole about the size of a looney in the centre which is protected by eight pegs. The round white or black and red checkers are propelled by the index or middle finger across the board where the opponent tries to knock them off and sink into the twenty hole. It is a fast-paced game of dexterity and skill and every farm home had one or more boards at the ready, kept slippery by generous applications of talcum powder or corn starch.

Our family was particularly good at crokinole and we were never allowed to be partners when playing at the competitive winter parties. I remember winning the prize for top male score at one of these events and receiving as my reward a tube of shaving cream. I was nine years old.

When city folk picture farm life of the past, they imagine that social events were made up of jolly hay rides, sleigh rides, horseback rides and buggy rides. Whenever any of this riding was done, it was seldom for pleasure. Certainly, if you managed to snatch a few hours of leisure, the last thing you wanted to do was harness up the horse again.

Today our farm families watch the same television, listen to the same music and dine in the same restaurants as anyone else. They belong to curling teams, little theatre groups and go on sailing vacations. In many rural homes, you'll still find a home-made bagatelle or crokinole board, a well-thumbed euchre deck, a doll's cradle lovingly carved from a pine stump or a game with no name at all, just something the "folks" always played.

PEARL HARBOR

As far as I know, the Bonisteel family invented "peckers." I have certainly never seen anyone else play with them.

They are made from two round pieces of wood an inch and a half thick and a foot long with a sharpened nail inserted in one end of each. The best pair I ever had was made for me by my older brothers from sawed-off sections of a shovel handle using pitchfork tines in the ends.

You sit on your sled on a long patch of ice and propel yourself forward by thrusting the peckers simultaneously into the ice on either side, and pushing. On a crisp cold day, when the ice is hard and smooth, incredible speeds can be obtained.

Our creek ran from the north-east corner of the woods, down through the pasture fields, skirted the barn and ducked through the tunnel under the CNR railroad that divided our farm in half. This meant a clear distance of about two miles without fence or any other hindrance. With winter's freeze, the creek varied between six and twenty feet wide and sloped slightly southward. Seated on a sled with your knees tucked under your chin and your arms pumping at your sides, you enjoyed a most thrilling home-made sport.

I very clearly remember one cold Sunday in early December 1941, the 7th to be exact, when I had spent half the day pecking on the creek. Hours of whipping around the trees in the sugar bush and manoeuvring the curves through the pasture had left me arm-weary and sweaty-cold.

I deposited my sled outside the back door of our farmhouse and vaguely wondered why no one called me for lunch. As the warmth of the wood-heated kitchen enveloped me, I saw my parents press close to the old battery radio and heard the voice of a sombre announcer repeating news bulletins.

"What's up?" I asked.

"The Japanese air force has attacked Pearl Harbor," answered my mother quietly.

"Where's that?"

"Apparently it's somewhere in the Hawaiian Islands."

In response to my blank look, she explained.

"The Hawaiian Islands belong to the United States. President Roosevelt has declared war against Japan. Canada will, too."

Even with two brothers enlisted, one already in Europe, the war seemed a long way away. Now, to me, it was just across Lake Ontario. Later that evening, as the setting December sun turned the entire western sky to scarlet, I put my sled and peckers into the woodshed for overnight safe-keeping. I don't recall ever taking them out again.

Fun-time changed after that. My favourite radio programs, "Tom Mix" and "The Lone Ranger", gave way to news broadcasts about Nazi U-boats trying to invade the east coast and Japanese Canadians being herded into detention camps on the west.

Childhood games took on a different complexion. At Christmas, instead of Snakes and Ladders, bob-skates and hand-knitted mittens, I was given model destroyers, dart boards with pictures of Tojo and Hitler in the bull's eyes and packets of War Savings Stamps. There was no more time for "pecking" on the ice or swinging on rope trapezes in the hay

mow – we now spent our time collecting tin-foil, metal cans and used
fats to be taken to the Victory Depot
in Trenton. I was never sure what was
done with these items but bombs
were mentioned a lot.

I'm a real Scrooge at Christmas. Not the Scrooge of
"Bah Humbug!" penurious ways or the kind who is
tortured by ghosts, but the Scrooge after his
transformation, described by Dickens as a man who
"knew how to keep Christmas well, if any man alive
possessed the knowledge."

As long as I can remember, Christmas has
always had a magical charm that makes me tingle
with excitement from the moment of realization that
the wonderful season is on its way.

It usually begins on an early December
morning when I step out of the back door on my way
to the barn or garden when something in the air – a
fresh smell from a crisp breeze or a change in the
tinkle of a frosty wind chime – seems to say "it's
coming." From then on, my days and nights are filled
with thoughts of the Christmas to come and the ones
I've had.

I have always believed in Santa Claus. He has
been a part of my whole life. As a toddler, my
imagination was fired by constant readings of A *Visit
from* St. *Nicholas* and it never occurred to me to
wonder how this fat little man could possibly get
down our crooked stove-pipes, since we had no
fireplace. He always appeared at Christmas concerts
at both school and church with treats for us kids.

Even when times were tough, a package of candy or a small toy was under the tree done up in a different kind of wrapping paper that could only have come from the North Pole.

CHRISTMAS

At this time of year, we hear the two most common complaints about Christmas. "It has become too commercial" and "It starts too early and lasts too long."

It's true that for some the Christmas season has become a big end-of-the-year sale that begins the day after Hallowe'en and ends with half-priced greeting cards on Boxing Day. But that's the Christmas of frantic last-minute shopping, competitive decorating and obligatory entertaining. Of all times in our complex lives, Christmas should be anticipated with pleasure, savoured and enjoyed when it's here, remaining gentle on our minds for months after.

The idea of Christmas as a desperate binge followed by the inevitable hangover is a relatively recent phenomenon beginning, I suspect, around the same time as the first television commercial told us what other people were buying. Prior to that we set our own agenda.

When Christmas gifts were made by hand, preparations began early. It never spoiled the surprise to see your mother knitting mittens, socks, scarves or toques since you didn't know which member of the family they were for. And, if your father was spending extra hours in the basement or garage during the fall months, you were smart enough not to go near. Many a bobsled, doll's house or hobby horse was lovingly handcrafted when time permitted.

Christmas wasn't crammed into a few frantic days. Its magic touched many other parts of the year. Before electricity made its way to rural areas, bringing strings of coloured lights and plug-in plastic Santas, house and tree decorating were year-round projects. The tin foil sides of tea packages were saved to wrap cardboard stars, strips of crêpe paper were woven into balls and streamers. The prunings from grape vines were kept for wreath-making. The tree itself was often spotted in the woods during the summer and, as you watched it grow and fill out, was a constant reminder of the joyful time to come.

The smells of Christmas are what I remember most from earlier days. A farm kitchen has a unique odour any time of year, with home-made bread, burning firewood and the inevitable orphaned baby animal being nursed in the warmth of the cook-stove. But as the year progresses, more exotic scents pervade. Cloves, cinnamon and ginger, coupled with the whiff of dried apricots and grated tangerine or coconut, were the delicious clues that Christmas candy-making was well underway. Oranges were the big treat for us kids. What a luxury to have a whole bowlful sitting on the sideboard and of course the special one in the toe of your stocking. Even today, the smell of an orange being peeled at any time of year will set jingle bells tingling in my head.

As I look through old scrapbooks of family recipes, I'm reminded that Christmas food preparation began many weeks before the big day. One recipe for mincemeat, made with chopped suet, two pounds of raisins, two pounds of carrots, apples, mace, brandy and wine says, it's better to "store in a stone crock for four months." A plum pudding concoction simply states, "make anytime of year. It will keep indefinitely." A 1774 recipe for Yorkshire Christmas Pie uses one each of the following: a turkey, a goose, a partridge, a pigeon, a hare, plus any woodcock, moor game and wild fowl you can get. It also includes four pounds of butter and the crust takes close to a bushel of flour. This recipe, from colonial Williamsburg, was often sent to England as a Christmas gift. Considering the means of transportation in those days, you can bet this wasn't whipped up at the last minute.

Before credit cards turned us into a buy-now, pay-later society, people actually saved what they could in advance to buy Christmas presents. The Christmas fund was a popular feature of the work place where a few dollars were taken from the pay cheque each week and accrued monthly interest until December. This savings-bond type of deduction was a weekly reminder of the Christmas joys to come, with no guilt or post-holiday debt.

Some people feel that Christmas should be over as soon as the turkey bones go into the soup pot. Once the tree is unloaded, they can't wait to get back to normal. Too bad! Christmas has an afterglow that can light our way well into the new year. The pleasure of giving, renewing friendships and the sheer joy of having fun with the family, should not stop when the decorations come down.

Whenever I meet people who think Boxing Day was invented to pack away the previous day, or who can't wait to vacuum up the tinsel, I tell them I'm glad they didn't organize the first Christmas. They would have been very disappointed. The wise men didn't even arrive until January 6th.

One Christmas morning, when I was about six, my older brothers had taken one of the feet from a slaughtered veal calf and with a long pole made a myriad of impressions up the snowy slope of the back shed and across the roof leading to the chimney. I was thoroughly convinced that this represented the reindeers' "pawing and prancing of each tiny hoof." I remember one year, even later, when my older siblings told me that no matter where in the house I hid my stocking, Santa would find it. I naïvely asked them to help me hide it.

Many years later, when I started in radio, I always volunteered to work the Christmas shifts. Not only did this allow the married staff members to spend the time with their families, but it meant I was able to program all the wonderful Christmas music and enjoy the special programming. On Christmas Eve, we would carry a carol service live from a local church, then join the NBC radio network for the midnight mass from St. Peter's in Rome. Sometimes this would continue until 3:00 a.m., giving me time for a nap in the manager's office before signing on the station at 6:00 a.m. for our Christmas Day shows.

In the fifties and sixties I worked at CKTB in St. Catharines, Ontario, and was responsible for producing all the holiday programs from noon on Christmas Eve until early Boxing Day. This meant a minimum of twenty-four taped half-hour shows featuring the stories and music of Christmas. Management had decreed there would be no commercials on these broadcasts, only sponsor identification at the beginning and end. Well into the seventies, long after I had left, the station continued running them and it was fun, when living in Toronto, to spend my own Christmas listening to myself from the Niagara area station.

While at that station, I was also the local Santa Claus. Each year, beginning about the third week in November, children would be invited to come to our studios and, by putting on the "magic headphone," contact Santa at the North Pole. Five or six children would file in with their parents each day and be given a candy cane to help calm them, while another announcer played "aunt" or "uncle" and put through the radio call to Santa. A sound effects tape provided the squeaks and squawks of static as the children sat wide-eyed in breathless anticipation.

"Hello ... this is station CKTB calling station XMAS at the North Pole ... (*squeak, squawk*)... Hello ... hello...."

From a temporary studio set up in the basement of the station well out of sight, I would respond: "(*Squeak, squawk*)... Ho, ho, ho... Hello... Ho, ho, ho... This is XMAS ... is someone calling Santa?"

Working from file cards that had been previously filled out as to names of brothers and sisters, pets, friends, hobbies and school work, I would Ho, ho, ho my way through conversations with each child, ending with the inevitable, "Have you been good this year?" and "What would you like me to bring you for Christmas?"

It was a very popular program for all ages. Children at home would listen with rapt attention, hoping they would get a chance next year. Business men confessed they planned their office departure so they could listen uninterrupted on their drive home. I still meet people today, now in their thirties, who tell me they were on the program as children and for them that was the *real* Santa as opposed to the ones they saw in department stores, on street corners or on television.

Though the guest list was always filled well in advance, an extended Christmas Eve broadcast was always done for children of staff members. That is when my own three children, Mandy, Steven and Lesley, would take their turn.

Lesley was always well organized and explicit about her list, spoke up well and thanked Santa for talking to her. Mandy was a little trickier. One year I knew from discussions at home that she wanted a sewing basket with all the accoutrements to make doll clothes; in fact one was already wrapped and hidden in our closet. On the air, and with the stores closed on Christmas Eve, she changed her mind.

"Ho, ho, ho ... and I understand you want me to bring you a sewing basket, Mandy."

"I've decided I'd sooner have a Moon Baby

doll."

"But sweetheart, Dad ... I mean, Santa, has already packed a sewing basket for you, Ho, ho, ho."

"Well unpack it, I want a Moon Baby doll."

"I'm sorry Mandy, the elves have closed the workshop and I'm leaving in a few hours. I'm afraid you're getting a sewing basket, Ho, ho, ho." That might have been the year Mandy stopped believing.

When Steven was three, he couldn't talk quite straight and only his family was able to understand him. The "uncle" that year was having a difficult time.

"I'm sorry Steven, would you repeat that? Get right close to the microphone and tell Santa what you want."

"I wanna *no nubble de nubble de no.*"

"Ho, ho, ho ... don't worry, Santa understands ... you want a snow shovel to shovel the snow. I'll see that you get one."

I still have many of the tapes that my children did on those Christmas Eves so long ago. Each year we get them out and my grandchildren renew their belief as they hear their parents talking to Santa.

I love the carols, the family get-togethers, the rereading of Dickens, Moore and Wilde's "The Happy Prince," but most of all I cherish the telling of stories that rekindle memories of other Christmases when the spirit of this wonderful season touched our hearts forever.

A Christmas Story

A CHRISTMAS STORY

Usually, when you live on a "mixed" farm, you can count on a few dollars from at least one source, even if other crops or pursuits fail. But the fall of 1944 in this area, at least on our farm, found our family approaching Christmas with no ready cash. Oh, we had enough to eat and we certainly could count on a plump turkey or chicken for the festive dinner and of course we had our own Christmas tree. It was just that there was no money for the extras.

Despite this, my father told my mother to go ahead and buy what she needed since the friendly merchants in Trenton would give us credit until after the holidays. Our ace in the hole was the woodlot. As soon as we got a few inches of snow, we would go into the woods and cut enough firewood to sell and pay off any debts incurred.

A week before Christmas, the snow started. Big, fat flakes that just kept piling up until the fence tops disappeared. Two days before Christmas the snow plough came down our dead-end road and turned around in the barn yard. It was a large wooden "V" loaded with boulders and was pulled by a four-horse team. The driver gave the horses a rest while he stomped the snow off his boots and came into the kitchen for a cup of hot coffee.

"They've got it a lot worse back around Stirling," he said, "more wind there. Some drifts over eight feet high. A few farms have been snowed in all week. By the way, are you selling any wood this year? Sam Barton told me to ask you if I saw you. He's right out and looks like he might have a pretty cold Christmas."

Sam Barton lived on the ninth concession with his wife and four children. He worked the old Homer place on shares and often bought a few cords of wood from us, usually later on in the New Year.

"We haven't started cutting yet," my father answered. "It would be too green to burn this year if we did. I could sell him a couple of cords out of our pile in the woodshed to get him by for awhile. Can we get into his place with the truck?"

"Yep. Should be all right. I ploughed his lane yesterday. You'd better get it back there tomorrow, though. If this snow keeps up, there's no telling how long you'll have."

And so it was on the afternoon before Christmas, my older brother Bert and I piled two stacks of dry split wood, each eight feet by four feet by four feet onto the stake body of the old Fargo truck and started out through the still-falling snow for the ten-mile trip to the Barton place. The truck's heater never worked well, but we were bundled up warmly and the cab was small enough that body heat was sufficient.

Bert played a mean harmonica and seldom went anywhere without it and, while my singing voice left a lot to be desired, I knew all the words to most songs. As we made our way slowly through the thickening snow, we butchered every tune on the current hit parade and assaulted every Christmas carol that came to mind.

It was almost five and we had turned on the Fargo's one good headlight by the time we spotted the Barton mailbox and drove up the snow-filled ruts of his lane. Sam and his wife, as well as the four noisy youngsters, made us feel like the relief of Dunkirk as they greeted us warmly and began to unload our precious cargo. When we finished, Sam asked Bert how much he owed, and my brother said, "Same as last year. Dad said not to charge any more just because it's dry. That's twelve dollars a cord and a dollar for gas."

I was thinking twenty-five dollars would certainly help Mom pay off what she owed for Christmas presents when I heard Sam say, "To tell the truth, I'm a little short this year. All I can spare is twenty dollars." Bert hesitated. Mrs. Barton looked embarrassed and hopeful at the same time as she said, "Let me give you a nice capon. It's already dressed and ready for the oven. My chickens were the only thing we had any luck with this year!"

"That'll be just fine, ma'am," said Bert.

I waited until we were out of the driveway and turned toward home before I said, "Dad's going to be some mad that you're short five dollars. And the last thing in the world we need is a chicken."

"What was I supposed to do?" asked Bert, "Put the wood back on the truck?"

The snow was still falling in earnest and a cold east wind had started piling drifts diagonally across the road. The truck, now without its weighty ballast, was skidding dangerously as the wheels carved new tracks in the pale glow of our single headlight. The windshield and windows were becoming thick with frost and we took turns scraping clear a small peep-hole on the driver's side.

It was at the corner of the fifth concession, still about five miles from home, where we went off the road. The back wheels swerved over the edge of a hidden culvert and we slid silently and deeply into the snow-filled ditch. There was no point in racing the engine and pushing was out of the question. We had to get help.

"The Creighton place is a little over a mile west," said Bert. "He'll have a tractor to pull us out. You'd better come with me. It'll be warmer walking than sitting in the cab."

We had only trudged about a hundred yards through the storm and I was thinking what a cold, miserable Christmas Eve it had turned into when we saw a faint light coming from the window of a small house off to the side of the road.

"Who lives there?" I shouted over the wind.

"I don't know," answered Bert, stopping and peering through the trees that lined the front yard. "I think it used to be an old tenant house, but somebody has fixed it up. Let's give it a try."

We were just about to knock on the door when Bert said, "Look!" Through the curtainless window I saw the strangest sight I had ever seen in my fourteen years and one I recall clearly even now, many Christmas Eves since.

An old man – bald except for a grey fringe over

his ears, wearing faded red long johns, was dancing spryly around the room – but he was dancing with a dog.

A handsome, well-groomed collie had both front paws planted firmly on the man's shoulders and was awkwardly but purposely striding back and forth. We could hear the music then and saw a wind-up phonograph in the corner of the room with a large flat disk revolving. Bert and I looked at each other, then back down the road where the truck was fast becoming invisible, and finally knocked on the door.

We heard the music stop and slippered feet shuffle to the door. It was opened wide and we felt the warmth of a roaring wood fire hit us as the man beckoned us quickly inside.

"Our name is Bonisteel," Bert said, "Our truck has slid into the ditch at the corner. I was wondering if you had a tractor I could borrow to pull it out."

"Sure have young feller. Got an Allis-Chalmers in the shed behind the house should do the trick. Take off those coats and sit for a minute first. You must be frozen. Don't worry about your boots."

As he motioned us to a slip-covered hobo couch to one side of the fireplace, I took off my coat and glanced around the room. It was small but neat. In the centre was a kitchen table and two curved-back chairs. A rocking chair was pulled up near the fire. A large kitchen cupboard dominated the far wall and the other three were hung with framed calendar prints of mountain ranges, seascapes and floral arrangements.

"How about a hot drink?" he asked. Without waiting for an answer, he took an earthen jug and some glass tumblers from the cupboard and put them on the table. Grabbing the poker from the hook over the fireplace, he pushed it deep into the red coals below the burning logs. He turned and smiled at us.

"Wasn't expecting company. Not many people stop in here. My own fault, I guess. Rose and I never made many friends out here. Oh well, it's too late now." He stood with one hand on the poker and stared at a small photograph over the mantle. It showed a laughing woman with thick long hair, head thrown back, eyes bright and full of humour.

"We moved here over three years ago from the Maritimes when I retired from the shipyard. Always wanted to get a small farm. Rose had a real green thumb ... grew vegetables. Didn't make much, but we were sure happy!"

The end of the poker was glowing red now. He removed it slowly and plunged it into the jug on the table. A hiss of steam erupted and filled the room with the smell of apple cider. He poured us each a glassful and took his to the rocking chair.

The first swallow of the warm liquid seemed to bounce off my empty stomach and brought tears to my eyes. I felt little tingles in my brain and realized that it certainly wasn't this year's crop. I glanced sideways at Bert and saw him smiling appreciatively. He was not the stranger I was to hard cider. The old man finished his drink in one, long thirsty gulp and absently poured himself another. He poked the fire needlessly.

"She died. Died two years ago. Just like that." He snapped his fingers, but no sound came. "Not a day goes by but I miss her. Like an ache it is. Sure miss her at Christmas. It was a special time for us. Didn't pay much attention to the religion part of it, but the love part was sure there. Maybe it's the same, I don't know. We'd make presents for each other, decorate the place with some crêpe paper and always had a roast goose or chicken. I can make a real good stuffing.

"I got good memories. Some minister came by after and said not to worry because Rose wasn't dead, she was living on in heaven. I guess he meant well. I know Rose is dead and the only place she lives on is in my memories. Maybe that's what heaven is ... memories."

A log fell in the fire and sent a shower of sparks up the chimney. This seemed to rouse him from his reverie and he noticed both his glass and Bert's were empty. I was still taking small sips from mine and thinking the warm room was making me woozy. "There's plenty more," he said.

"Thanks, but I'd better get the truck out," answered Bert. Then, with a glance at the old man, he said to me, "You stay here and keep warm. I can yank it out by myself."

"Be careful of the crank, it kicks sometimes," the old man said as Bert buttoned his coat and went out the door.

With his glass refilled, he sat down by the fire and in a minute continued talking. His dog yawned and stretched closer to the fire.

"She was an English girl. Met her on Christmas Eve at a dance in Liverpool during the last war. I couldn't dance worth a hoot but she showed me how.

Would you mind putting that music back on?"

I went over to the phonograph and gave the handle a couple of turns, then dropped the arm over the edge of the record. The music started as I returned to the couch.

"That piece is called 'Greensleeves.' It's an English tune. We danced to it that first night. It's a waltz you know. Rose taught me how to make a box pattern with my feet. One-two-three ... one-two-three. We laughed so much. We got married while I was still in the navy, then after the war we came to Canada. Got off the boat in Halifax and decided to stay there. Lots of good years. Never had kids. Didn't seem to matter. Had each other."

The music stopped and the needle made a scraping sound in the last groove. He started to sing in a low, halting voice.

> Alas, my Love! Ye do me wrong
> To cast me off discourteously:
> And I have loved you so long,
> Delighting in your company.

I went over to the machine, lifted the arm and turned off the turntable.

"I heard they made a Christmas carol out of that piece," he said. "Makes sense. It's always been a Christmas song to me."

He was humming now and staring into the fire. I heard the tractor come up beside the house and sputter to a stop in the shed. Bert came through the door with a blast of cold air. The old man didn't even look up. I put on my coat.

"Thank you very much," my brother said. "We really appreciate your help." There was no reply from the figure who rocked and hummed by the fire. Bert took from under his mackinaw the fat capon and set it on the table beside the cider crock. "Goodbye," we both said as we backed out the door. The dog thumped his tail twice on the floor in acknowledgement.

The snow was tapering off and, by the time we got to the second concession, had stopped completely. Neither of us spoke on this final leg of our journey. As we started down our own dead-end road, the moon broke through and shot blue shadows over the snow-drifts.

I could see the lights ablaze from every window of our farmhouse as we drew near and I thought of Christmas Day, just a couple of hours away. With the snowfall ended, my other brothers and sisters and my aunts and uncles would be able to come. There would be laughter and games and shouts of joy as we opened our almost-paid-for presents. Loved ones, together.

As we turned up the lane towards the yellow lamplight spilling over the snow, Bert had his harmonica out again. He was softly playing "What Child Is This?"

Acknowledgements

The newspaper columns appearing here were originally published in the Kingston *Whig-Standard*. They are reprinted with the kind permission of the publisher, Michael Davies.

I would like to thank Anis and Ernest Harrison who, besides being the finest father- and mother-in-law a person could have, read the manuscript and gave valuable suggestions and friendly criticism.

My appreciation to John Pearce, Jill Lambert and Maggie Reeves of Doubleday Canada for their editorial assistance and professional expertise.

I would especially like to thank my wife Jane without whose love, support and encouragement this book would never have been written. Besides, she edited the whole damn thing.

About Scraperboard

This unique medium originates from 1880, when it was introduced in Europe. Scraperboard, or scratch-board, is a chalk-clay surfaced board on which ink can be applied. When the ink is dry the surface of the board can be cut with a knife or blade to produce a line drawing. By drawing in the traditional manner of the nineteenth century, the scraperboard artist can capture the visual effect of the woodcut or metal engraving.